A GLASS
HALF FULL

A GLASS HALF FULL

LAURA HEFLIN

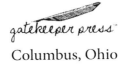

Columbus, Ohio

A Glass Half Full: How Tuning Into God's Truths Can Change Your Perspective And Change Your Life

Published by Gatekeeper Press
2167 Stringtown Rd, Suite 109
Columbus, OH 43123-2989
www.GatekeeperPress.com

Library of Congress Control Number: 2022932099

ISBN (paperback): 9781662924682
eISBN: 9781662924699

Dedication

To my husband, Chris, and my kids, Scarlett and Carter, who make my glass feel that much fuller every day.

Back of Book/ Book Summary

Are you sprinting past all the colorful roses on your path in life? Have you been so focused on life's thorns that you have lost sight of all the beauty that God has placed right in front of you? Maybe today you find that you are so entangled and burdened by life's hardships that you put all your focus and attention on the negative. But guess what? God doesn't want that for you. He wants to reveal to you His glory even on the hardest of days. Now yes, for a while your circumstances might very well stay the same, but your perspective doesn't have to. The truth is we all have blessings in our lives that sometimes we just can't see. But God has a knack for teaching us how to stop living color blind. We just have to be willing to ask Him.

Contents

Introduction

So, what? So what if I choose to view this world and my life through rose-colored glasses? So what if I choose to stop being anchored by all the negativity and hardships that life inevitably brings and instead choose to rise above it and see each day and each moment in a new light? Yes, my friend. The fact is that life will sometimes bring us pain, sadness, despair, and stressors in waves that often make us feel as if we have been abandoned in the sea alone without a lifeboat in sight. We seem to get hit by a wave that shakes us and knocks us down only to get back up to meet another wave, towering over our heads and getting ready to knock us down once again. I have been guilty in the past, and even some days still am, of giving in and allowing my spirit to sink straight to the bottom of the ocean. Overwhelm and discouragement take over and I'm tempted to just roll over and play dead hoping that I'll wake up one day and life's hardships will be over. But that's just not how life works. In life we are dealt playing cards. Some may be the ones we wanted and others, well, not so much. But the fact of the matter still stands that these are *our* playing cards. So, it's up to us to play them well and not just toss them to the center of the table, throw our hands in the air, and give up. The truth is, anyone in life that you may view as successful and admire as a person of strong character with enviable vitality still was dealt a few cards in their life that I promise you they didn't want. From Anne Frank, the Jewish captive, Martin Luther King, Jr., the constantly hunted civil rights leader, Joni Tada, the quadriplegic to Paul the Christian martyr in the Bible, I can vouch for each and every one of them and tell you that their lives at times were simply downright hard. Yet, they still chose to shine their light in this dark world and not be paralyzed by their circumstances and what many would call it their "unlucky hand" of playing cards. You see, the thing is that you and I were put here on this earth for a purpose and the devil knows that. He wants us so badly to give up and burn out before we finish the race. He wants us so badly to see the world as dark and gray and full of sadness and despair. He wants nothing more than to blind us from all the beauties in our life and in the world that God has put right in front of our very eyes. In Isaiah 40:31 it says, "But those who hope in the LORD will renew their strength. They will soar on wings like eagles; they will run and not grow weary, they will walk and not be faint."

Do you remember the disciple Peter in the Bible? When he kept his eyes on God he was able to accomplish something many of us would never even dream of doing. He walked on water! But the second his eyes started focusing on the water underneath his feet guess what happened? He started to drown! So yes, choosing to look up to the Lord instead of down at our seemingly never-ending problems can and will in fact renew our strength and allow us to live a full life instead of one encased by fear and depression. Choosing joy every single day and striving to find tiny specks of golden light within the darkness is *key* to living out our best life. But it's a *choice* to do so.

Sure, we can choose to focus on the negative, but really, where is that going to get us? I'll answer that for you. It won't get us anywhere. In fact, the more we choose to hyperfocus on our dilemmas, the more we work against ourselves and end up walking backwards. Listen, I have had my share of hardships in this life and I will be the first to tell you that this life is hard and sometimes downright exhausting. I won't pretend it's not. However, I made a choice long ago to prayerfully and wholeheartedly choose joy each and every day (though trust me, I still struggle to do this some days because after all, like you, I am human). But nevertheless, seeing the beauty in my life is something I always strive to do. Why? Because I absolutely refuse to be a vulnerable target for the devil. God says that if we remain hopeful, which, by the way, requires optimism, He will renew our strength. Yet, if we stay stuck in our problems and the sadness and negativity of this world, the enemy has a much greater chance of knocking us down further. So darn it, I'm going to rock my cat-eye, rose-colored glasses today and show the devil what's up! What about you?

A Message to Those Struggling with Depression: "You Are Seen"

Hey, you. Yes you, stuck in the pits of depression, I see you. I see how hard you are trying to pull yourself out of the gray, dark, and despairing reality you're in. I see you, reading this book, trying your very hardest to find the answer, "the key," to getting out of this hole. And I have to tell you, though there are many ways I know I can help you shift your perspective through the lessons that God taught me that I will share with you in this book, *you may need professional medical help like I did.* I know. I didn't want to hear those words either. I didn't want to face the fact that I, a holistic nutritionist, would ever need medication to find healing. It took me hitting a very dark place, and one I'm not proud of, to face the fact that my PTSD from infertility in combination with postpartum hormonal ups and downs had caused a chemical imbalance in my brain that I couldn't shake and that didn't allow me to see the light no matter how hard I tried. I was in a never-ending fog, and though I had exhausted every single holistic remedy possible, I still suffered. I spent ten years of my life suffering with severe depression and anxiety, and for the longest time I didn't even admit it, not even to my own husband.

I tried my best to fake it till I made it to no avail. Chemical imbalances within the brain can be debilitating and it wasn't until after a couple months of being medicated that something finally clicked and I was able to break free from these chains that had entangled me for nearly a decade.It was then that I got my life back and I no longer just survived, but I started to thrive. It was then, a few years after I became a mama, that I gained the mental capacity I needed to start really living out my best life and soak up all of the beauty around me. It was then that my brain allowed me to finally see the glass as half full. Now, I am not a doctor, and I am in NO WAY saying that medication is the right route for you, but what I AM telling you is that you owe it to yourself to find out which route is. My hope and prayer is that this short chapter will hopefully give you the permission that maybe you have been seeking to go get help and speak to someone. You can exist without your mental health, but you can't fully live out this beautiful thing called life. So, I am writing these words to give you hope and tell you that no matter how dark of a place you currently find yourself in, with God you can rise above it and there is beauty to come. You just may require a little modern-day medical help, counseling, or hormone tweaking to get there, like I did, and that's okay. I'm sending you all the love in my heart and I promise you, there are better days to come. Now, if you're ready, let's dive further into discovering what it takes to obtain this glass-half-full perspective, shall we?

Note: If you would like to learn more about my postpartum journey and hear more of how God carried me through my mental health struggles, you can check out my last book *Mama, You Still Matter.*

The Definition of "True Joy"

"The deepest craving of the human soul is Jesus."
—Pastor Daniel Floyd

"True joy." What is it and where can it be found? I'll cut straight to the chase and tell you that it's not found where most of the world keeps looking. True, unwavering joy is found in the person of Jesus Christ. It's not found in a promotion or a raise, a drop in the scale, a new relationship, another glass of wine, or in a new purchase. These things aren't necessarily evil or ungodly by any means, but they will never truly fulfill one's thirsty soul. True joy is found in Christ *despite* our financial, fitness, job, or relationship status. It is a joy that surpasses all understanding. It is a joy that to some looking at us from the outside, may even find odd or out of place if our current circumstances are less than "ideal." We will have hard days, weeks, months, or maybe even what seem to be years, but regardless, the truth still stands. Our circumstances don't define us. God does and He wants to teach us how to find freedom and joy through Him and Him alone. When we get the idea of "joy" misconstrued, we instantly lose our peace because our circumstances are always waning. We will inevitably go through highs and lows throughout our lives, but our confidence and joy are found in the Lord and the knowledge that His love for us is never-changing and never-ending. News flash: The enemy doesn't want you to discover this joy that the Lord has to offer. Instead, he wants to distract you from its true meaning on this earth by constantly making you feel less than or at a deficit in some way. I'll be honest and tell you that I sometimes fall prey to the enemy's deception and find myself guilty of feeling this way. For example, our culture has taught us that "shopping therapy" is the perfect bandage for a hard day. "A new sweater, a new lip gloss, or a new book? That'll make me feel better, won't it?" In the short-term, yes, it'll distract me from the chaos in my life but it won't bring me the lasting joy that I know the Lord will bring me. I don't know about you, but I don't want joy that has to be bought and that can flee at any moment. I want joy that isn't fazed by my day-to-day circumstances and life's trials. I want the type of joy that to the world, doesn't even make sense. The beautiful thing is that God makes this joy available to each and every one of us! But it doesn't come without prayer, and it doesn't come without a change in perspective and a little work on our part. If we learn to look at our glass as half full instead of half empty and we choose a spirit of thankfulness over one of graveling, we might just start experiencing life in a way we never have before. If we choose to not settle and really embrace who God made us to be, we might start partaking in this "full life" that God keeps talking about throughout the Bible that can't be taken from us and can't be bought. I know that I sure want to live out a life like that. Don't you?

"Have To" or "Get To"?

"Have to" is an obligation. "Get to" is a privilege and a gift."
—Anonymous

Do you remember the seven dwarfs in the original *Snow White*? Do you remember the song they sang and how obnoxiously cheerful they seemed to be as they went about their work? Yeah, I know. I really don't get it either. I mean, it's not like their job as miners was exactly luxurious and it definitely was repetitive work, so why did they cheerfully sing that tune all darn day? Well, my guess is that they made a choice somewhere along the way to look at their work as a blessing instead of a burden (except for Grumpy of course). Instead of grumbling as they went about their work, I can bet that they chose a "glass half full" approach instead.I think I can speak for the majority of adults and say that this can be extremely hard to do at times, especially when life seems to be one never-ending to-do list. Honestly, adulting can be downright hard! But still, as with anything in our lives, we have to again *choose* joy and choose to look at the glass as half full if we really want to obtain joy. Yet, how often do we find ourselves begrudgingly going about our days, frustrated at the fact that we have so much to do? How often do we find ourselves wishing that we could just torch that growing pile of laundry staring at us in the face and toss those dirty dishes out the window? (I may have strongly considered both once or twice.) How often do we wish our kids could just do their own homework or bathe themselves without our help, or that dinner or that report for work would just magically get done without us having to do it? Is life just one long, never-ending chore? I think it sure as heck can feel that way. *That is, if we let it.* But guess what? It doesn't have to feel that way! In fact, I am a firm believer that if we retrain our way of thinking and the words we use, it can make all the difference in the world. If we start looking at what God asks of us daily as a blessing instead of a curse, we may just discover a new joy that we didn't know existed. One thing I have really strived to do in my thirties has been to change up my choice of verbs from "have to" to "get to" and what a difference it has made in my everyday life!

A shift in our perspective and in our choice of words takes practice but it is something that can truly change our lives. God says He wants us to live out our lives fully and one of the best ways to do that is to develop more gratitude within our hearts. But *how* do we build up a greater feeling of gratitude towards our everyday life? Well for starters, I think we have to start by looking at the tasks the Lord has set before us (as mundane and repetitive as they may be) as a *blessing*. Yes, a blessing! Look, friend, I know you are worn out and I know you are tired. *But I guarantee you that whatever tasks you are called to do today, someone, somewhere would be exceedingly grateful to be able to "get to" do what you "have to" do today.* Someone, somewhere wishes they had a house to clean, kids to help do their homework, or a job to work that pays their bills. In Thessalonians 5:18, God commands us to "give thanks in all circumstances; for this is the will of God in Christ Jesus for you." If you notice God didn't command us to just give thanks when sitting on the beach in a lounge chair, when life is feeling easy and breezy. No, instead we are commanded to give thanks daily, regardless of our circumstances or how much or how little we "have to" do.

As someone who has struggled with depression for the majority of my adult life, I am all too familiar with two happy hormones, dopamine and serotonin. In case you don't know, these are our "feel good," "get up and get things done" hormones that I am sure we all feel we could use a bit more of. Did you know that it has been scientifically proven that practicing gratitude throughout our day naturally raises each of these hormones? Yes, that's right! Simply shifting our inner dialogue from "I *have to* do these dishes and laundry and clean up after the kids" to "I *get to* do these dishes and laundry and clean up after the kids" can actually make you a happier person overall! Perspective is everything, my friends! Each day that we "get to" wake up once again with breath in our lungs is a new day that we "get to" be the hands and feet of Jesus. There is a reason that addiction in our culture is at an all-time high. Though there are many reasons, including some that are clinical, I believe that in many cases it is because so many are lost and searching for a new "high" or excitement that will give them the dopamine or serotonin boost their brain is so badly lacking. Now please hear me clearly once again. As I already stated at the beginning of this book, mental illness is very real. I am a victim of depression and I thank God every day that we live in a time that medical intervention is available to us. That being said, even on medication, I can tell you very transparently that if I didn't practice gratitude daily, I myself would be searching for something to bring me joy apart from the life that God has blessed me with.

Alcoholism, drug addiction, pornography addiction, sex addiction, shopping addiction, you name it, can, in many cases, stem from that feeling of emptiness one feels without the joy of Christ in their lives. As Christians, God is waiting to help us vanish our negative, ungrateful perspective and spirit and shift it to one of gratitude. When our life feels void of joy and blessings, it's only natural as human beings to go searching for it elsewhere. But God has SO much more for us, and He has so much joy waiting for us on the other side of a grateful heart! We only have to pray for our eyes to open so that we can see all of the hidden treasures in our lives that are right in front of us. *We don't "have to" do anything in life, my friend. No, we "get to" and if we want unwavering joy in our lives, then we have to stop getting this confused.*

DIVE DEEP:

- Do you feel that you "have to" or "get to" do all that is required of you throughout your day?

- Write down five tasks that you need to accomplish today starting each one out with the words "I get to" and then fill in the blank.

- Say a little prayer today and ask God to shift your perspective as you go about your work today. Pray that He will help you view your tasks as blessings instead of burdens.

The Time Is Now

*"What a wonderful life I've had! I only wish
I'd realized it sooner."*
—Sidonie Gabrielle Colette

"I've had cancer, so I now celebrate my birthday for an entire month instead of just a day," she told me. Rebecca was celebrating her eighteenth birthday the day she received the call that changed her life. I can only imagine that getting the news that she had cancer on the very day she was celebrating her newfound adulthood was shattering and life-altering. Yet, she chose to not let her cancer diagnosis define her. She beat it only for it to come back again three years later. Then, she fought hard to beat it again, but this time she had to go through a new type of cancer treatment that left her very sick and depleted. She chose to document her journey openly by sharing her story on social media along with her "Bald Is Beautiful" Facebook photo album for the world to see. The day the doctor called her with her results, she not only was given a new cancer diagnosis, but, to her, she was given a whole new outlook on life. Her perspective on life and her definition of what it meant to be blessed drastically changed.

A couple years later, after fully recovering from her second battle with cancer, she met her husband and they fell in love and got married. Shortly after, she became pregnant with her miracle baby boy. Throughout her pregnancy, she had several major complications and went on to have a total of five operations before her son was born. As hard as this was, Rebecca still didn't lose sight of the beauty in her life and the appreciation she had for the blessing growing within her. She had beaten cancer twice and was being given the opportunity to be a mother, which, at one point, she didn't know would ever be possible. Now Rebecca is the mama to an adorable and vivacious little six-year-old boy who she often shares pictures of with the caption "my whole world." It's funny how hard times can shake us, shape us, and make us appreciate the little things that so many take for granted, isn't it? Depression and anxiety were, for me, my cancer. I struggled and suffered with it for ten long years. For a decade, I saw gray. I was numb and the life that I once knew and loved was being lived out in front of me, and yet, I wasn't able to participate in it. Instead, I was forced to sit back with my hands tied and watch others live it out. I struggled with my mental health from the time I turned twenty-one years old, but I unfortunately spiraled even deeper after my daughter was born when my postpartum depression hit.

It was a time in my life that I was *supposed* to be happiest, but instead I was in complete agony. Depression attempted to crush my spirit but with God, I was able to stand strong through the storm and come out on the other side. I held onto and often repeated the verse in 2 Corinthians 4:8–9 that said that "we are hard pressed on every side, but not crushed; perplexed, but not in despair; persecuted, but not abandoned; struck down, but not destroyed" over and over. Truly, without the Lord, I can't honestly tell you that I would still be here today. But God. He showed me the way, and He carried me through.

Man, how my perspective of "just another ordinary day" has changed! These days, I wake up and thank God that He has given me another chance to live mentally healthy once again. I am no longer paralyzed by depression and anxiety, and I can't even begin to put into words how amazing it feels to even type this declaration. Of course, I would have rather not experienced such inner turmoil and sadness for that decade of my life. But I know that because God allowed me to go through that storm, I can now view the colors of my life with a greater saturation than I ever could have before. I know how blessed I am to not just physically be here on this earth but to mentally be truly present for each day. I know the harsh reality of depression and anxiety, and I know how many beautiful years I missed out by having to sit on the sidelines. *So, these days I get out onto the field and I play hard.*

You see, I have discovered that if we want to really live out our best life, we have to remember that not a single day is "ordinary" but instead, it is an incredible opportunity to *do* something, *be* something, or *say* something that will make a difference in this world. Circumstances and hardships like cancer, depression, and infertility taught my friend Rebecca and I to remember how precious each day really is. Truly, no one is promised tomorrow and each day is such a gift. So, if you wake up to yet "just another day" don't think for two seconds that you aren't blessed. The reason you woke up today is that yes, even though you may be in the midst of depression or hardship, *God isn't finished with you yet my friend!* He has something or many things left for you to still accomplish or experience here on this earth.

So always be on the lookout. Prayerfully go about your day and ask God to direct your steps and shine light on the path He wants you to take. If an opportunity to do something presents itself, pray about it and if God gives you the green light, then dive all in. If you are given the chance to speak out about something, speak loudly. If you are given the opportunity to support and come alongside someone in their trials, don't back down. God wants to use you to make a difference. So, make it your goal to live each day as if it could be your last. Though that may sound like a pessimistic, depressing way to live, that mindset helps us live with the urgency and drive we need to keep from settling for "just another ordinary day." Love harder, smile bigger, laugh louder, and live with a passion in your soul that lights up others around you. Don't make the mistake of thinking that you can start living large tomorrow. We are on borrowed time, my friend. The time to start really living is *now*.

DIVE DEEP:

- Do you finding yourself waiting for tomorrow or for the "perfect time" to start pursuing you dreams or take the next step?

- Do you truly believe that God has a purpose for you here on this earth? What do you think that purpose is?

- Pray and ask God to give you the opportunity to do, say or be something today that will make a difference in the life of another.

The Beauty in Surrender

"Hope deferred makes the heart sick, but a longing
fulfilled is a tree of life".
—Proverbs 13:12

Each of us are dealt cards the moment we are born that dictate our life's circumstances, experiences, highs, and lows. Sometimes when things aren't going our way, it's easy to ask, "God, why? Why these cards? Why was I the one picked to carry these burdens?" I know I have asked this several times throughout my life, particularly while going through infertility.

I'll never forget a few years back, when I was sitting in a Panera eating lunch with a friend and pouring my heart out to her about my desperation for a baby, when, after a few minutes, she kindly interrupted me and said, "Laura, you are letting this take over your life. If God doesn't bless you with a biological child, you WILL be okay. You have to be willing to accept it if that's not His plan for you."

"Ouch!" I thought. Here I was having recently suffered what was then my fifth miscarriage and all I was looking for was a safe place to vent, but I found myself being lectured. I was upset. I was hurt by her comment, but now looking back I see that this friend of mine was right. She *was* wanting to be a safe place for me and she actually did know how I was feeling because she had gone through infertility and the adoption process a couple years prior. She *did* want to give me room to grieve but she wasn't willing to sit back and just watch me spiral.From the outside looking in, it had become evident to her just how engrossed I had become in trying to "fix" my situation and reshape my life to fit the mold I had always imagined it to be. It had always been my plan that by five years into marriage, we would at least have one baby under our belt, or maybe even two. But it just wasn't happening for us and I started to go from sad to mad. My view of life in general became so skewed and I had developed tunnel vision that was so fixed on my pain and what I *didn't* have that what I *did* have became blurred. At that time in my life, infertility took up my every waking moment and thought. When I wasn't Googling fertility tips, I found myself envying and comparing myself to others and crying out to God asking, "Why me?"

Did I have a right to be upset and anxious about my situation? Absolutely, I did. I am human after all, and I'll be the first to tell you that infertility downright sucks. But allowing myself to spiral and wallow in sadness and self-pity was doing me way more harm than good and my friend saw that. My relationship with God and my husband had become strained, my job I once loved became a burden, and my enthusiasm for life had been squashed.

Now, looking back, I can see that God wasn't answering my prayers with a "no" like I thought He was but with a "not yet." He was working in my heart and molding me into the mom my children needed me to be. But at the time all I wanted to do was stomp my feet and huff and puff because it wasn't happening when *I* had planned. I can honestly tell you that because I chose to spend so much time focusing on the fact that I didn't have a baby, I stopped appreciating the already existing blessings in my life. I missed out on so much because I had stopped living in the present. Instead, I was living in a hypothetical daydream of what I wished my life was like.

I eventually did receive my rainbow baby. But do you want to know when? It was after I declared out loud to myself, my husband, and to God that I was done trying to control this situation and I was choosing to be at peace that if our last fertility attempt didn't work we would adopt and stop trying. I wholeheartedly told the Lord with open hands, "I will accept it if your answer is no, even if I don't understand it and even if it leaves my heart shattered. I want your will for my life and not my own. May your will be done."

I declared these words out loud on a sunny, Sunday afternoon drive with my husband and it was the following Thursday that I found out I was pregnant with my daughter. The moment I read my lab results on my computer at work, the country song "Don't Let Me Be

Lonely" by The Band Perry came on and I know that in that moment God was telling me it was time for the void in my heart to be filled. It says in Proverbs that "a hope deferred makes the heart sick. But a longing fulfilled is a tree of life." I knew in that moment that by surrendering my plans to Him for my life and choosing to accept whatever He had for me, I was then made ready to receive His blessing. That blessing came in the form of a little six-pound eight-ounce baby girl whose due date just so happened to fall on Mother's Day 2014. Was that just a coincidence? No, I don't think so. I think God knew what He was doing all along.

As hard as it was, I see now that God used my infertility for His glory and as a way to shape me into the woman I am today. God taught me that true joy, beauty, and blessings are found in our surrender to Him. When we pray and ask God for something, He will always answer us with one of three answers: "yes," "no," or "not yet." I'm so thankful to say that my prayer for biological children was eventually answered but if God had chosen to tell me "no" instead of "not yet," I know He would have carried me through and had a reason for it. I know that as heartbroken as I would have been, life would still have kept going and I would have found joy and purpose in another way.

So, if you find yourself in the waiting game, holding onto every waking moment, just waiting for your prayers to be answered, then I want to encourage you to stop.

Stop holding on so tightly to what you think you need in your life and start changing your prayer to "not my will Lord but yours." When you do, I can promise that profound miracles and blessings will be bestowed upon you. Some of these blessings may be just the very things you prayed for, and some may be something or someone you didn't know you needed. But you will never know what it is or what they are if you keep trying to dictate your plans to God. Pray with open hands and then keep on living. *Don't shut out the blessings right in front of you as you are waiting for a new one to be born.* Learn to let go and let God and then just watch how He moves. Learn to surrender your hopes and dreams to God and then watch the beautiful things He has planned for your life unfold!

DIVE DEEP:

- When you pray, do you pray with open or closed hands? Are you afraid of what God's answer will be?

- Do you truly want God's plan to play out in your life or are you more stuck on your own plan?

- Are you more focused on the blessings you currently have or the blessings you wish you had?

A Dream Is a Wish Your Heart Makes

"When we can't dream anymore, we die."
—Emma Goldman

I grew up nonchalantly putting my shoes on the wrong feet, rocking a messy braid, and going throughout my days without a care in the world. I remember swinging for what seemed like hours on our old wooden swing in our backyard while leaning back and looking up at the clouds. I was a dreamer and from the second grade on, I would come up with story after story after story in my head and write them down.

"You have a gift, Laura," my mom always used to tell me. At the time I don't think I knew what she really meant, but all I know is that I kept writing. I don't really know why or how I fell in love with writing but what I do know is that it happened at a very young age. I was a passionate dreamer and I wrote down whatever words came to my mind the moment they would hit me. I made my siblings sit down and listen to my stories over and over whether they liked it or not. Then later, throughout middle school and high school, I would write poem after poem and story after story in between (and often during) classes.

Writing woke something up inside of me and I wrote every chance I got. When my classmates were sitting in biology class learning about the human body, I was scribbling down words to another story or another poem. This, I'm sure, had something to do with my low C average I received in that class at the end of the year. Thankfully, however, my A in English helped level out my overall GPA. Sure, I could sit happily and write loads of papers and reports but standing in a lab and dissecting frogs? Yeah, no thank you. I'll pass.

Growing up, I fell in love with writing and because I did, I told myself that I would never stop. But then, something happened. I got older and life got harder. By the age of eighteen I was married to my high school sweetheart, and we were as in love as we were broke. At that point in my life I just didn't feel that I had time for something as frivolous as writing poems or stories anymore. "It is time to grow up and face the real world," I thought. So, for three entire years I stopped writing and slowly I felt depression sink in. I realized over time that something inside me was missing but I just kept suppressing the feeling because c'mon, who really has the time to just sit around and write?

Despite all the good in my life at the time, I felt an emptiness inside of me that I can't really explain. This feeling of emptiness lingered until one day on a whim I decided to start a blog. Honestly, at the time, I didn't think anyone would read it and for a while, no one really did. But I didn't feel that it really mattered because I wasn't really writing for others. I was writing for me and I can't even begin to tell you how happy it made me feel to finally be doing what I loved once again. *I learned through this experience that the moment we stop using our gifts and pursuing our passions, something on the inside of us dies. So, we can't let that happen.*

I promised myself then that I was never going to give up on writing again and here we are, three books later. And what do you know? God turned a little girl's favorite pastime into something that has now impacted the lives of many others and it's in no way my doing, but His. I get emotional just thinking about all the DMs I have received from complete strangers who have said that my books and my blog have encouraged them and helped them find freedom. Truly, my obedience to Him in utilizing my gifts and pursuing my dream to become an author paid off in a bigger way than I could have ever imagined; and I know the same will be for you if you obediently use your gifts as well.

The thing is, we all have the ability to utilize our gifts and be dreamers if we choose to be. But it often takes great bravery. Look back in history. Anyone who ever made an impact had a dream deep within them and they had to use their God-given gifts, passion, and courage to see them through. Martin Luther King, Jr., even started his famous speech bravely announcing to the world, "I have a dream." And just look at what became of that!

You and I were each given dreams, gifts, and passions for a reason and they make us who we are. If we lose sight of them, life will keep going as it always has but we will no longer really be living it. Instead, we will be living as a hollow shell of a person who just goes through the motions instead of a person who is living fully alive. *How can life appear beautiful when we allow our passions and dreams within us to die?* It can't.

We have to use the gifts God has given us because even though they may seem minuscule to us, to God, they aren't! Each of us makes up the body of Christ and we were all given unique gifts, talents, and passions for a reason, oftentimes unbeknownst to us. If we passionately pursue them and utilize them instead of shutting them away, then God will be able to use us in extraordinary ways and together we can change the world for the better.

Do you really want to live a glass half full kind of life? Are you sick of just going through the motions and seeing gray? Then stop thinking that using your gifts in any stage of life is optional. Stop telling yourself you don't have time for them or that they are meaningless. Instead, honor God by pursuing the passions that He implanted in your heart and use your gifts. When you do, I can promise that life's beautiful colors will start to reappear and that spark that has felt so dim deep inside of you will once again be set ablaze.

DIVE DEEP:

- In which area or areas do you believe that you are most gifted?

- How often do you take the time to use this gift or these gifts?

- Pray and ask God today for more opportunities to use your gifts to better His kingdom.

Learning To Unapologetically Shine

"When something robs you of your peace of mind, ask yourself if it is worth the energy you are expending on it."
—Kay Arthur

Sometimes I think that we fall into the trap of believing the lie that we can't shine our light, spread our joy, or exude positivity because others in our lives and throughout the world are suffering. If you feel this way, you aren't alone and I understand why. Misery loves company and it always has. One day, about a year ago, and when COVID had just had yet another surge, my husband and I were on a little weekend getaway, and we were out golfing when I shared a quick Instagram story of us smiling together with our golf clubs.

Within minutes, I had a DM from a follower telling me that I shouldn't be sharing a picture of my husband and I having fun when there was so much suffering going on in the world. "Hold up. Did I just read that correctly?" I thought. I showed the message to my husband riding in the golf cart beside me and he confirmed that I did. I honestly was dumbfounded by this woman's message because to me, it should be quite the opposite. I mean, when darkness and sadness is engulfing our world, why can we not be the ones to bring a little light back into it? Why not share that happy moment, that uplifting Bible verse, that funny meme, or that new delicious recipe you just made? In my book (literally speaking), we should or at least feel free to.

The truth is, you don't need permission to be happy in life when others aren't. In the same way, those around you don't need permission to be joyful when things seem to be going south for you. I think it's incredibly sad that we live in such a judgmental culture that loves to speak first before considering the fact that they aren't seeing behind the scenes and that they really don't have a clue what that person has or is going through.

That one spring day when I received that hurtful DM, my first thought was "if only she knew." If only she knew that I had finally found freedom from my ten-year battle with deep, dark depression and that I finally had rediscovered happiness and traded it for the darkness that once seemed to swallow me whole. If only she knew how hard my husband and I had worked on our marriage to get to the point we were at. If only she knew how many pictures I had to look back on in my life that were nothing but a reminder of the hollow shell of a person I once was. If only she knew. But she didn't know. Yet, she was quick to judge me behind a screen and then proceed to tear me down. I try and not let things get to me but if I am being honest, her message that day, for whatever reason, really did.

Life will always have hardships, pain, loss, and sadness but it doesn't mean that you have to be encased in it. It's up to us to search hard amidst the darkness and find the light and then spread it. If those around you and those you love are currently in a valley and life seems to ironically and *finally* be on the up and up for you, that is okay. It doesn't mean that you can't sympathize with them and cry with them. It doesn't mean that you can't love and encourage them through their struggles and care about what they are going through. But your story is your OWN. There will for sure be hardships in every one of our lives. But again, if you happen to be at a high point in your life (and I am going to bet that you, too, have fought through hell to get there), don't hide it. In fact, I believe it's essential that we share good news and the blessings God has sent our way because by doing so, we are glorifying His name!

Thinking back to when I was pregnant with my daughter (my first rainbow baby) eight years ago, for instance, I couldn't help but share picture after picture of my growing belly. I couldn't help but share picture after picture from each of my ultrasounds (I had multiple as I was with a high-risk doctor) and later, each of her infant milestones. And I am 1000% *sure* I annoyed some people, including some friends and family in group chats on the receiving end, as I was constantly pinging their phones. But yet, I did so unapologetically because I wanted to share my little miracle with those I loved and with the world. And speaking of spreading joy, who doesn't love a cute, toothless, smiley baby, right?

In the Bible God says to "rejoice! Again I say rejoice!" He commands us in the Bible to rejoice and shout from the rooftops all the amazing things He has done! If we only talk about life's hardships and struggles, I think we are giving the devil more attention than he deserves. In the same way we are given freedom to mourn, we are also given full freedom to rejoice unapologetically. So don't shy away from positivity just because of your surroundings. Frankly, and since the fall of Adam and Eve, there has been pain and suffering in the world and that's not going to change. So don't shy away from sharing good news or joy just because those around you aren't in the same place you are. On the flip side, don't fall into the "must be nice" vicious trap of jealousy when things aren't going so great for you either. Because really, that nasty green color isn't a great look on anyone, if you ask me.

Celebrate what God is doing in your life and in the life of others and let the negativity and criticism fall to the wayside. *Shine your light when the world is demanding darkness and shine even brighter when others so badly try to extinguish your flame.* Use their negative darts of criticism as fuel for your fire! This world undoubtedly is a hard and, oftentimes, very dark place and it so badly needs your light! Joy and positivity are contagious and therefore, when you choose to shine, you will light others up around you. I wholeheartedly believe that the more we all do this, together we can illuminate this dark world and make it a better place. The world could use a little glimpse of heaven and a little less hell on this earth these days. Am I right or am I right? So, I urge you to unapologetically choose and spread joy today, my friend. The world is waiting to see you shine!

DIVE DEEP:

- Do you ever avoid posting or sharing something out of fear of what others my think?

- Think of a recent moment or experience that brought you joy. Now, thank God for it.

- When others share their happy news or pictures are genuinely happy for them or do you find yourself envious of them?

Protecting Your Achilles Heel

"The thief comes only to steal and kill and destroy;
I have come that they may have life, and have it
to the full."
—John 10:10

As Christians we have a God-given conscience that eats away at us when we know we are dabbling in sin. God really wants to use us and give us that unexplainable joy that we've been talking about but the thing is, we really can't obtain this joy with a pricked conscience. In fact, there's nothing that can steal our joy faster than that feeling of guilt that leaves us in a constant state of unrest. It's no secret that the enemy wants so badly to lead us astray from the path God has for our lives. He knows that by tempting us with something we struggle with and by making it seem innocent and attractive, he has a chance to keep us from experiencing true joy and freedom.

Whether it's lust, alcohol, drugs, gambling, or something seemingly more innocent like gossiping or stretching the truth, he wants us to fall prey to it. I can tell you from personal experience that, like clockwork, the moment I begin a new book, I feel Satan's attack. My kids seem to grow horns, my husband and I seem to be at odds, my workload seems to become overwhelming, anxiety seems to increase and the temptation to give up writing and instead find solace in something more appealing creeps in. Yes, my struggle against the enemy's attack is very real and so is yours.

Satan loves to distract us from our purpose and from what God has for us to do here on this earth. Oftentimes though, it's hard to admit that our conscience is being pricked or that we are struggling with temptation. It's easier just to pretend like we are unphased by it and just push it under the rug. But I'll be the first to tell you that no one is immune to the enemy and his attacks, and he knows exactly where our Achilles heel is. Therefore, it's up to *us* to protect it by bringing it to God and asking Him for a hedge of protection.

Allow me to drive the point further home by telling you a little backstory. I'll cut straight to the chase and start by telling you that for as long as I can remember, I have been a hopeless romantic. In the early days of my marriage I would find myself escaping reality through reading romance novels back to back in order to get the fulfillment I was looking for in my own marriage. In those days and when the honeymoon phase was over, things seemed to become extremely challenging. We were young, married and in love but we were financially tight, we were in the thick of school and starting a family seemed to be an unachievable dream. Our marriage was very strained and the enemy knew it and we constantly seemed to be under attack.

I'm ashamed to admit that instead of focusing on what I needed to do at that time to change and better our lives or marriage, I would nitpick and scrutinize my husband, often in my head and sometimes even out loud. Each night that we argued or adulting proved to be too hard, I would lay in bed and turn to a fantasy romance novel that would allow me to escape my reality and allow me to feel that "high on love" feeling that I thought marriage was supposed to be all about. I turned to these novels to numb myself from reality and Satan would distract me from addressing the issues within my marriage and the issues within myself. After a few years, I can honestly tell you that I became addicted to the high I would get from reading about these sexy heroes who would rescue and romance these women, and I started to resent my husband for not measuring up. I know. It was awful and it was unfair. "But okay, wait Laura. Are trying to tell me that your secret Achilles heel and downfall is or was romance novels?" The answer is *yes*, I am, and for me personally, it turned out to actually be a very big deal.

Secular romance novels had a hold over me in the same way I would imagine pornography would over a man. I read these novels the most over the first three years of our marriage, which, ironically was the same time period that I had also stopped using my gift of writing. Go figure. What seemed to be just another innocent download on my Kindle app turned out to be my Achilles heel and Satan's attempt to strain my marriage and distract me. Not only was my husband not filling my love cup emotionally in my eyes, but these novels also made me overanalyze my husband in a very unfair way and look at my glass as half empty.

Satan knew that these romance novels were dangerously attractive to me in the same way that another beer would be for an alcoholic. I don't think it was a coincidence that as soon as I finished one novel, an advertisement for another one would somehow magically pop up right in front of my face. The enemy is sneaky and He knows how to knock us down when we have strayed away from our relationship with God and we are distracted by things of this world. But how could I have gone three years as a Christian neglecting my marriage and filling my head with trash? It's simple. Satan had dangled bait to lead me away from the Lord and my focus on my marriage and I took it.

Eventually, God got a hold of me and I confessed to my husband the hold these books had over me and how sorry I was for neglecting our marriage. Instead of facing our trials together head on as a team, I chose to be distracted and whisked away into a romantic fantasy world. When I finally made the decision to only read Christian romance novels and break away from any that weren't honorable to Him (sorry *Fifty Shades of Gray*, you didn't make my reading list), I felt a weight lifted off my chest. I felt and witnessed my marriage get stronger and I felt the Lord nudge me to pick up writing again. By prayerfully asking the Lord to protect my Achilles heel and help me avoid temptation, my joy was restored and my conscience was once again clean. I no longer felt the heaviness that I would feel lying next to my husband each night reading these novels that I finally realized were not only putting a damper on my joy and spirit, but were also harming our marriage.

I finally felt free, and it was in my confession to the Lord and to my husband that my joy was restored. Sometimes even still, the enemy tries to tempt me to escape to another romantic fantasyland when my life or marriage hits a rough patch, but I now know to quickly say a prayer to ask God for strength and firmly tell him to flee; and then, he does. The enemy knows that God's got me and that he no longer has the power to outsmart me and lead me down that old path that I know leads to nothing but an unquenching thirst.

So, friend, what about you? What is your Achilles heel? We all have one (or several), so please don't even try to tell yourself that you don't. There is such a strong power in identifying what it is and bringing it to the Lord! Remember, it says in John 1:9 that "if we confess our sins He is faithful and just to forgive us." We are told to bring our struggles to the One who created us. And the beautiful thing is that when we do, God will guard us from the devil's schemes and he will flee! *But first, we must start viewing healthy boundaries as blessings because really, that's what they are.*

God placed boundaries in our lives to offer us a freedom and a joy that the pleasures of this world will never be able to give us. He gave us boundaries to protect us because He loves us and wants us to live out our best lives. So, embrace them and welcome His protection. Identify your Achilles heel, regardless of how big or small it may seem, and then bring it to the Lord. When you do, I promise that He will give you the strength to break away from its chains and they will no longer entangle you. And take it from me, that feeling of freedom in itself will offer you a "high" that nothing in this world could ever give you.

DIVE DEEP:

- What is your Achilles heel?

- What boundaries have you put into place to help guard you against it?

- Spend a minute or two today to ask God for extra protection in this area.

Clocking In with a Smile

*"Whatever you do, work heartily, as for the Lord
and not for men, knowing that from the Lord
you will receive the inheritance as your reward.
You are serving the Lord Christ."*
—Colossians 3:23–24

You and I both have dreams and aspirations for our own lives as I believe we most certainly should. I am sure that, like me, at a certain point in your life, you have spent some time daydreaming about what you think it would be like to reach your professional potential and what it would feel like to score your "dream job." Maybe, it is something that God has planted in your heart that you know without a shadow of a doubt He is calling you to do. Maybe it is something that even though you don't know when or how, it will one day be your reality. You can just feel it in your bones and so you live with joyful anticipation of the future and what is to come.

But wait. *What about the here and now?* What do we do when we know in our hearts what God is calling us to do in the future but we are currently feeling "stuck" in a waiting period and in a job we don't love? What do we do when we wake up and begrudgingly have to drive ourselves to a job day after day that we would gladly quit in a heartbeat if it wasn't for the stack of bills on our countertop reminding us of how badly we need the money? Is life just supposed to, for lack of a better term, "suck" until we finally reach our professional potential and hit our dream job or fulfill something that we believe God is calling us to do?

Some may think yes, but I wholeheartedly want to tell you that the real answer is *no*. Life doesn't have to "suck" when we are feeling stuck or until we reach the next, best level and chapter in our lives. In fact, I guarantee that even if you were to score your "dream job" tomorrow, there would be something about it that you would realize you didn't love so much and something that you would wish you could change.

But look, I get it. If you are in this waiting period, I want you to know that I have been there and I know it is not always an easy place to be. Let me just remind you that I was married at the ripe age of eighteen, fresh out of high school. I had just started college so my work options were quite limited at the time, as I did not yet have the degree that was required to become what I wanted to become (which at that point in time I really didn't even know what that was. I only knew that I wanted my own fancy desk somewhere in the respectable corporate world). During my freshman year, I started working at a rundown daycare with some not-so-friendly and unprofessional people and I barely even made minimum wage. It wasn't easy and it for darn sure wasn't what I wanted to do long term but yet, I was determined to find joy in it and try my best to show up with a smile each day.

Why was I determined to do this? Well for starters, I realized that more than likely this job was going to be my new reality for a while, so it only made sense that I make the best out of it. I mean what do you do when life gives you lemons? You make lemonade, of course (or maybe a batch of raspberry lemon muffins like I just made for my next *Live Healthy With Laura* photo shoot. Yum!)! Anyways, as far from my dream job as this position was and despite the fact that it didn't pay much, it *did* pay the bills so I couldn't just quit. I was, as many would like to say, "stuck in the mud."

Some days, I frankly dreaded being around my gossipy, rude coworkers. Most of them were unkind to me because I was the young "new girl," and I often would get thrown under the bus for mistakes they made because I was an easy target. It wasn't fun and I quickly realized that after a few weeks of working there, I was most likely never going to be friends with most of my coworkers or be accepted by them. Yet, I felt God asking me to shift my focus on *who* I was serving each day despite *who* I was working with.

Truly, I grew to really love those kids that I got to care for. These babies needed to be loved and nurtured and even though I could have chosen to be miserable day in and day out, and just show up and go through motions, I again shifted my focus to *who* I was serving (most days, that is). God gave me an opportunity to be a light in these young children's lives, some who one could very easily tell had hard home lives. I found joy in putting smiles on their faces each day and giving them the love that they craved and needed that I was so blessed to have received as a child. I also found joy in practicing my mothering skills in joyful anticipation of the babies I knew I would one day have and the babies I knew God was preparing me for.

After a couple of months, the one thing I decided that I would stop trying to do was find approval in the eyes of my coworkers who obviously had no plans to accept me and that in itself was a huge weight off my shoulders. I chose to instead prayerfully go to work every day declaring, "I am going to be a light in this world and a blessing to someone today!" It also helped me to remember that by serving others, I was serving the Lord and that gave me so much joy. Now don't get me wrong. I still had my "off days" where I had to drag my butt off to work. But once I was there I tried to focus on those I was impacting and that made a big difference.

Hear me out, okay? Even if we aren't getting validated or seen by others (or are unfairly being thrown under the bus, as I once was), God sees us behind the scenes and He sees our hearts to serve. Therefore, we can rest easy knowing that, regardless of our occupation or status, if we give it our all and put our heart into it, we can rest easy that night knowing that we reflected Christ into the world that day and God is pleased with us. We can then let that in itself, be our source of joy!

You may not think anyone is watching you, but I promise you that they are and I promise you that you are making a difference in this world (regardless of how far up or down the corporate ladder you are). So please, keep showing up and not just physically but wholeheartedly, because the world needs *you* and what you have to offer! When you do, God will bless you with a unique joy that the world and your current job status could never give you!

I learned this early on in my young adult life. Now fast forward to today, thirteen years later, and I can happily tell you that I love, love, love my job! I love helping others better care for themselves and feel their best and I love the people I get to work with! But even so, I still have some hard days. I still have days that I just don't want to "adult" anymore and I would rather not put in the work because I just get tired like anyone else. However, what always gives me back my stamina is remembering *who* I am serving which makes all the difference in the world.

Today I want you to know that even if your current occupation is far from enjoyable or ideal, there is a reason you are where you are, in the job you are in, with the people you are with. So find out what that reason is and then make that your focus when you clock in each day.

Remember, if you shift your focus to the people you are serving instead of those you want validation from, you may just start viewing your work as a blessing instead of a burden.

Regardless of what job you currently hold today, whether it be in the corporate world, in school, or at home with your babies, I am a firm believer that you absolutely can find joy in *any* job God has put in front of you *if* you stop working to please man and start working to please the Lord. He is watching you each moment of every day and He sees your heart. So, despite how much you currently claim to love or detest your current job or line of work, I challenge you to stop watching the clock. Stop just showing up counting down the minutes until you can leave and remember that God has you where you are for a reason, even if you have yet to discover it. Your dream job may very well land on your lap one day but don't make the mistake of coasting and missing out on the here and now. Find joy daily in *who* you serve instead of *what* your job status is and get ready to experience more joy 9 a.m. to 5 p.m. than you ever have before.

DIVE DEEP:

- Do you clock in with a smile or do you drag yourself to work and count down the moment until you can leave?

- List three positives about your job, even if you have to really dig deep.

- When you go to work, *who* do you serve and how could you serve them better?

Rest For the Weary

"Come to me, all who labor and are heavy laden,
and I will give you rest. Take my yoke upon you,
and learn from me, for I am gentle and lowly in
heart, and you will find rest for your souls. For my
yoke is easy, and my burden is light."
—Matthew 11: 28-30

Social media. It has been a part of our culture for years but for the longest time, I never really understood the hold it had on me. I never really understood how constantly scrolling and being plugged in impacted me and disrupted my mental health and my overall wellbeing. I never caught on to why and how it was stealing my joy and peace. The only thing I began to recognize was that it was. For the longest time, social media was what I would start and end my day with and for years I gave it an unnecessary power over my life and my emotions.

One day after I had just finished scrolling through my Facebook page, a thought hit me. *Maybe our brains and emotions weren't designed to take on the burdens and updates of the entire world.* Maybe part of my anxiety and ongoing feeling of unrest had something to do with how little I was in my own world and how much I immersed myself in everyone else's. Maybe my perspective of life was skewed by this never-ending reel that I began and ended my day with. News articles, happy announcements, sad announcements, memes, vacation photos, holiday photos, it all contributes to what I like to call "information overload" and it finally occurred to me that maybe it had been taking more of a toll on me than I realized.

If you think about it, years ago our ancestors weren't living in a sea of new content every day that required their brain to process new, sporadic, and extra information from the outside world. Aside from a little Sunday gossip, most families had the weekly paper delivered to their doorstep and that was it. They weren't logged on to the internet multiple times a day, inviting the problems and updates of the world far and wide into their heads and into their homes.

What I have personally found is that even if I intentionally choose to start my day with a thankful heart, my glass half full perspective can easily get knocked over in an instant when I start viewing the lives of others or read news I'm not emotionally ready to read or process. But how about you? I want you to ask yourself when was the last time spending thirty minutes scrolling on social media actually sparked joy and left you feeling uplifted? I want you to really think about that for a minute.

Coming from someone who is well aware of the pain and struggle that anxiety and depression can bring, I can honestly attest to the fact that I can count on one hand the amount of times that scrolling mindlessly on social media positively influenced my mental health. That may sound a bit extreme to say, but seriously, it's the truth. It may not necessarily depress me, but I have found that it always has the power to overwhelm me and keep me from living in the present with those I love. Life can be difficult and hard enough at times as it is. I don't need constant updates from social media contributing to it, at least not every day that is.

Now, please hear me clearly. I'm not saying social media or the news is bad by any means. Shoot, my business probably wouldn't exist without it! And I absolutely think it's important to stay informed about the world around us to a certain degree. But I do think we have to be extremely careful not to get sucked into the never-ending reel and emotional rollercoaster that social media can take us on. I will say it again. *You and I weren't designed to carry the weight of the world's burdens on our shoulders.* Yet, that's just what we are doing if we choose to start and end our day with news and social media.

Did you know that at the start of 2021, it was estimated that one out of three American adults struggled with depression? That is an astronomical amount and, if you ask me, that is not a number we should accept. Yes, COVID has, without a doubt, put a strain on all our lives but I bet that if social media and the news didn't exist or was only available to us for a small window of time each week, that number would look quite different.

One of the healthiest things I did during the pandemic is stop watching the news entirely. Yes, I completely stopped watching it. Why? Because I knew I was not in a healthy headspace, and I recognized that it was stealing my joy and triggering my anxiety. Thankfully, though, my husband had a news app on his phone and volunteered to update me with any groundbreaking news stories he thought I should know (but not when I first woke up and not when I was about to go to bed). Another thing I did was ban myself from scrolling through social media for a period of three months. Instead, I scheduled my *Live Healthy With Laura* posts ahead of time and I got on once a day for ten minutes in the middle of the day to check my notifications and my inbox, and then I would quickly sign off. I also moved my Facebook and Instagram apps to the fourth page on my iPhone so I wasn't constantly seeing the amount of notifications I had.

Because I did this, I cannot even begin to explain the weight that was lifted off my shoulders and how much my overall outlook on my life began to change. "But wait" you may ask. "You said you were put on antidepressants, so that must have been why you felt so much better!" But, nope. That wasn't it. Antidepressants helped me feel less anxious and blue overall, but I still had a dark cloud looming over me for months when I was still exposing my brain and emotions to social media and news updates multiple times a day. Remember, viewing new pictures, reading updates, whether good or bad, seeing new memes, and browsing news articles are all information our brain is required to process and it can only process so much information in one day before a fuse blows. Truly, It truly wasn't until after I made this change that I started really seeing the light once again and that I was then able to *be* a light once again for others. It was then that I regained the mental capacity and energy I needed to be present and to use my gifts and it was then that I began writing my first book.

I will say, though, that my family, consisting of my husband, my parents, and my five siblings and their spouses all have a group chat where we keep personal photos of our families and funny memes circulating weekly. We also have a group chat with my husband's side of the family and my best friends and I text often as well. But these texts and group chats don't drain me because I am only taking on new information and updates about my family and closest friends, instead of the rest of the world. And frankly, if someone is close to me and I am close to them, we won't need social media to keep us connected. Wouldn't you agree?

In the Bible God commands us to come to Him when we are weary. Well as I have just expressed, a couple years ago I was feeling extremely emotionally weary, so I prayerfully went to Him and He put it on my heart that my relationship and ties to social media needed to change. So I made some changes and man, am I glad I did! Even today, I still limit myself on social media to a certain degree. I only allow social media into my life in a very specific and controlled way that I know won't drain my emotional energy and I evaluate how I am feeling each day. I still blog weekly and check my notifications daily, but I hardly ever scroll. I have learned that my brain simply doesn't have the mental capacity to take on the rest of the world's highs and lows, and I would argue that truly, yours doesn't either, at least not multiple times a day. I get that maybe the restrictions I put on myself in regards to social media seem a bit extreme. Maybe the boundaries I need to remain emotionally healthy and positive are not the same boundaries you think you need and that's fine. But do yourself a favor and at least stop and ask God what boundaries you *do* need because if you ask me, we all need social media boundaries in some regard to stay emotionally healthy.

As I conclude this chapter, let me leave with you a few questions to ponder. What is your overall outlook on your life and the world around you? Is it all doom and gloom? Are you feeling overwhelmed and unable to see the beauty in your own life and in your surroundings? Are you constantly comparing yourself to others? Is your mind within your four walls with those you love, or is it more wrapped up in highs and lows and updates of the world outside? These are just a few questions I think we should all be asking ourselves often because really asking questions is the only way to gauge our mental health and to decide if social media is really blessing us or draining us.

This week I challenge you to take a pause and pray about your relationship with social media. If you discover that peace and joy in your life is lacking, I challenge you to then ask God to guide you in putting up protective boundaries for yourself as I once did so that your peace and joy can once again be restored. Remember that sometimes, all it takes is a few small changes in our everyday life for our perspective to shift and for us to once again be able to notice the beauty that is all around us. It was my experience a couple years back that by logging off, I was really able to start seeing the beauty in my life and that I was able to wholeheartedly say "yes" to tasks that God placed in front of me. Okay, enough about me. How about you find out what logging off, at least once in a while, can do for *you*?

DIVE DEEP:

- How much time do you spend on social media each day?

- Do you feel that social medial increases your joy or weighs down your spirit?

- What healthy social media boundaries could you set for yourself? If you don't know what they should be, pray about it and let God guide you.

Age Is Just a Number

"The older I get, the more I understand that it's okay to live a life others don't understand."
—*Aditi Sirvaiya*

Twelve years ago, Taylor Swift came out with the song "22." One of the lines in the song was, "Everything will be alright if we just keep dancing like we're twenty-two!" At the time that song came out I was twenty-one years old, young and married, and working hard in college and for my dad and his medical practice. To any onlooker, things from the outside looked alright, yet nothing felt "alright" as Taylor put it. In fact, I felt more lost than ever about what my true calling was and my struggle with clinical depression was at its most heightened point. I can tell you that on my birthday when I blew those candles out, nothing magically changed. There was nothing about turning twenty-two that made me feel more accomplished, less depressed, or less lost. Honestly, it really wasn't until I reached thirty years old that I really started to discover a joy that I had not discovered in my teens or twenties and that I was finally free from depression. It wasn't until then that I started to really discover my true calling.

Now, I hate to break it to you, but in the same way that there is nothing magical about turning twenty-two, there was really nothing magical about turning thirty either. Despite common belief, turning thirty does *not* always equal thriving. Nothing about that number, or any number for that matter, ever changed my circumstances. But God. It was simply just His ordained time for me to reach a certain high point in my life where He knew I was ready for several new and exciting doors to open. It was then that God decided I finally had the spiritual maturity and mental stability that I needed to further dive into and discover a new calling in my life: writing books that would reflect Him and bring encouragement to the world. And yes, ironically, I started writing books at the age of thirty with two, very young, very needy children and hardly any quiet time in sight. How different from my quieter days in my earlier twenties, right? The timing didn't make sense, I know, but God had His reasons. He knew then, I was ready.From a young age, though, I always did things a little strangely and in different time frames than those around me. I was born with loads of passion in my heart and an enormous amount of creativity in my head and I just couldn't for the life of me keep it in. As a toddler it has been reported back to me that I had quite "the gift to gab." In fact, at the age of two I couldn't even walk but boy, my mama said that I could I sit there and talk! Multiple specialist visits later, it was determined that I actually *could* walk. I had decided, though, that talking was more up my alley and I just so happened to be quite advanced at it! Plus, who wouldn't like to be carried around all day?

Anyway, my uniqueness continued and as a young child I would sit on the sidelines while others played and I would write stories instead. I was also "that kid" who once dragged her dad's briefcase around the neighborhood with a rope on a family walk claiming to onlookers it was my "dog" because in my imagination, well, it was. And let me tell you, it didn't take long for my parents to buy us a real puppy. No pressure right? Ha! Later in middle and high school I was that kid who would be staring out the window daydreaming and watching the birds during class while others took notes around me. And yup, I was that hopeless romantic girl who, at the age of eighteen, got married and *then* went to college.

I always like to think that maybe I got my uniqueness from my grandmother. She, too, was known for going about her life differently and in a non-traditional way. In fact, at the age of seventy-five, she decided she was going to finish her college degree. Though it didn't make sense to the world, she didn't care. It was her new calling and newfound passion to finish school, so she cheerfully and unapologetically walked across that stage with her children and grandchildren in the audience.

Now correct me if I'm wrong, but in our modern day culture, the average timeline for one's life in the twenty-first century is expected to look something like this: you are born, you go to preschool, elementary school, middle school, and high school, and then go off to get your four-year degree. At the age of twenty-two you graduate college and pursue your career. By the age of twenty-five you get married and purchase your first home. By the age of twenty-six you buy a dog. Then, by the age of twenty-eight, you start popping out a couple of kids and then you proceed to work a nine-to-five office job until you hit the age of sixty-five. Once you eventually retire, you have a few years left to pursue your hobbies, spend some time at the beach, volunteer and then, if you're lucky enough, you make it to the ripe old age of eighty-five and then, well? You die. That sounds about right, doesn't it?

But let me ask you a question. *What if you don't feel called to go about your life in this way?* What if, like me, you meet the love of your life at the age of fifteen and decide to get married fresh out high school at the age eighteen? What if you decide to forgo going to a traditional four-year college and disappoint some people in your life because you choose to pursue another avenue that God has placed on your heart? What if your calling is to stay home and keep house and raise babies? What if you feel called to move to Africa and pursue missions? What if you feel called to open a coffee shop or maybe write a book or start a band? What will others think?

The answer is that frankly, it really doesn't matter what they think. It only matters what God thinks and no, you actually don't have to always do things the traditional way. Ultimately, trying to follow in someone else's footsteps or stick to cultural norms can lead us down a very depressing road. Why? Because we aren't living out our full potential and following the plans the Lord has for us. Instead, we are more caught up in staying in line with what the world deems as acceptable or praiseworthy.

If life has taught me anything, it's that regardless of what the world believes or perceives, you are never too young or too old to be where God currently has you. *Don't let logistics, statistics, opinions of others, or cultural norms rob you of the joy and confidence that He has for you in this season.* God has amazing plans for your life, but in order for you to really recognize them, you have to shut out all of the noise and stop trying to measure up to the world's expectations of you. Others' approval might matter to us here earthside, but it won't matter when we get to heaven. So stop gauging your life's plans or timeline based on what you "think" the world wants to see. Instead, pray hard and ask God to guide you and then unapologetically walk daily in the direction that He is pointing you in. Also, remember, whether you are twenty-two, thirty, or seventy-five, it's never too early or too late to start that business, write that book, get that certificate or degree, run that race, learn how to cook, pursue teaching, ministry, or missions and become the person you were always meant to be!

I personally decided long ago that I was okay with being the "weird one" because it meant that I got to really live passionately and freely and live out my best life. I won't lie to you though and tell you that this always came easy. It required me to really do some serious soul searching and evaluate if I was living out of familiarity or out of obedience to God.

Let me encourage you too to take a minute every now and again to really evaluate if you are following God's unique plan for your life or if you are being held back by fear of what you believe others will think of you or by society norms. Really evaluate if you are playing it safe and simply doing what you think is expected of you. If you find that you are in fact playing it safe, then let me let you in on a little secret. *The enemy doesn't want you living large and making strides here on this earth. He wants you playing it safe and staying put where you are.* Don't play his victim by missing out on all that God has for you and all He has for you to do! Regardless of how many birthday candles are on your cake this year never believe for a second that you are too young or too far gone to do great things because that's nothing but a lie from the pit of hell. Instead, live in joyful anticipation for all that is to come and just think! What if this year is just the beginning?

DIVE DEEP:

- Do you ever find yourself believing that you are too young or too old to accomplish a dream that's within your heart?

- Do you find yourself making life decisions based on what you believe others expect of you?

- Are you playing it safe or are you brave enough to trust God and venture off on the rocky path?

It Could Always Be Worse

"Start each day with a grateful hear
— Psalm 107:1

There was a movie that came out once called *Ever After* that I, being the hopeless romantic that I was, would watch over and over growing up. Seriously, I was so obsessed with it that within a year after it came out, I think I probably had every line memorized. Now, I can't say that I remember each line to this day, but there was a line that I can tell you still sticks with me. *"No matter how hard life gets, it could always be worse."* This line was ironically said by the wicked, evil step-mother who didn't have Cinderella's best interest in mind at all, but still, she did speak a lot of truth in that moment.

You see, sometimes I think we get so emerged in our problems that all we see is our seemingly hopeless and exhausting circumstances and we really believe the lie that life couldn't get any worse. But then, you happen to hear on the news that an earthquake has hit on the other side of the world that has killed thousands and has left hundreds of families broken and without a home. Or maybe you are stuck thinking about how dire your money situation is and how you hate your job only to be caught at a stop light suddenly making eye contact with a homeless person who very evidently has neither. You get frustrated with your kids or your spouse and sometimes think, "Man, these people are draining the life out of me" only to see a post on Facebook of a friend announcing that she has tragically lost her husband to a tree accident in their yard. Then you scroll a little further to see a mom holding her baby's hand in the hospital begging for prayer and healing for her son's newfound leukemia diagnosis (remember how I mentioned scrolling almost always is triggering for me?). Yes, truly, life could always be worse and we have a lot to be grateful for.

For me, when I hear these stories, my whole perspective shifts and I think, "I *have* a home, a job, a husband, and healthy children to love on! So many people don't." Sometimes I think, "How could these people even keep living after what has happened to them?" But, even Job in the Bible who had everything stripped from him and who was left empty, broken-hearted, and crying out to God somehow found a way to keep living. So often, we are so blinded to what we have that by the time it's gone, it's too late to really appreciate it. Maybe if we shifted our way of thinking to, "yeah, this is hard, but it could be worse" instead of "my life sucks" we would start to discover the joy that God has for us and maybe start looking at our circumstances a little differently.

Once we become a Christian, God can promise us a freedom and a joy in our lives that is not of this world, but He can't promise us a pain-free ride. Life is hard and trust me, I get it. But we can't become victims to our circumstances no matter how hard they may be. Why? Because there is a reason you and I are still breathing. As I have already said, I know wholeheartedly that there is a reason God allowed us both to wake up this morning. Every day is a new chance and new beginning and enough of a reason to keep going even when life is hard. Just the fact that you and I are still here means God has more for us to do on this earth. If you find yourself paralyzed by your current hardships, I want you to stop and just look around at the world we live in.

Pain, loss, hatred, and strife have always been, and will always be a reality, until we reach Heaven. But really, God has so much joy for us here on this earth and He wants us to stop being slaves to our difficult circumstances. He wants us to brush off and break free from the chains of our hardships and give them to Him. So today, instead of focusing on all we don't have or all we have lost, how about we start focusing on what we *do* have? Do you have a car that runs? Do you have legs that work? Do you have a spouse or a family member or a friend that loves you and that you get to love in return? Do you have kids to hug? Do you have a roof over your head? Well then, *you have something someone else in this world wishes they had or maybe wishes they still had.* So my friend, listen up! If you are really after that glass half full shift in perspective then it's time to stop hyper focusing on all of the negatives and it's time to really dig deep. How about today you take a moment to write down ten things you are thankful for. Then, and as you go on into the future, remind yourself that no matter how hard life gets, it could always be worse.

DIVE DEEP:

- When hard times hit, is it easy for you to stay positive or do you easily spiral?

- Do you believe that even on a hard day you are still blessed?

- What is something that you are exceptionally grateful for today?

You Have Nothing to Prove

"Lions don't lose sleep over the opinion of sheep."
—Anonymous

I am the queen. I am the queen, that is, of sensitivity and caring too much about what other people think of me. I am, or should I say I *was*, the queen of letting others' criticism ruin and wreck my day. Honestly, I think it all stems from my childhood. From a young age I longed to be accepted and liked by others (but let me tell you, that cystic acne covering my face and back brace I was forced to wear didn't work in my favor). For as long as I can remember, I had an urge to people-please and gain satisfaction from those around me. Now, though it's not necessarily a sin to want to please others to some degree, unfortunately, at certain points in my life, this people-pleasing mentality caused me to care less and less about what God thought of me. I often stopped remembering who I was ultimately serving. Because I did, what do you think happened? I got burned. I got burned by others' rejection and lack of approval and my feelings were hurt more times than I could count.

Sometimes I would feel that I would "measure up" but then many times I wouldn't, and that feeling of rejection, whether in relationships or later professionally, stung. I can happily report, though, that today at the age of thirty-two, I now have a much tougher skin than I did in my twenties and teens, and I really have obtained that "God confidence" that the world can't shake . . . most days, that is. But there are still some days I struggle when someone's criticizing comment of me makes me think, "Ouch! That hurt." But those days are much fewer and farther between than they used to be.

I think the turning point in my life was the day a couple years back when I put myself out there on social media in the biggest and most vulnerable day. It was the day that I snapped a picture of my prescription bottles on my countertop and posted the truth: that behind the scenes, this bubbly, smiley woman everyone had been seeing on the outside had been silently struggling with depression and anxiety on the inside. It was also the day that I shared my struggle with postpartum depression and the day that I unapologetically let the world see the real me. And guess what? It was that very same year that God gave me the confidence I needed to write my first book. It was also the very same year that I achieved the most in my career. Yet, it ultimately wasn't my doing. I would never have been able to dive all in if I didn't have that "God confidence" the Lord gave me.

I think sometimes we put so much pressure on ourselves to "act the part" and try to follow in the footsteps of others who we deem successful. We start believing the lie that we have to act a certain way, be a certain way, and say things in just the right way to prove ourselves to others that we are worth their time and attention. When, in reality, what the world really needs is the most real, transparent, and unique *us* that we can bring! We have this idea of "success" or "achievement" in our minds and of what it looks like, and we feel pressured to perform. But can I let you in on something? *You actually don't have to prove yourself to anyone. You just have to show up, be yourself, and try your very best, and then just let God handle the rest (oh hey, that rhymed!).*

God sees your heart and knows you better than anyone, and when He feels the time is right, He will part the Red Sea and make the way for you to achieve greatness. And it won't be reliant on whether another person thinks you're qualified or worth it. But please hear me clearly. I'm in no way saying that you don't have to work your tail off to get where you want to go in life because you absolutely do. Ultimately, though, each goal we accomplish in our lives is only accomplished because God *allowed* it to be accomplished. Every low and high point in our lives has been part of our destiny. Every failure and every victory have been part of God's plan for us. He makes the way for us when He knows it is the right time and He gives us the strength we need to make it to each finish line.

Even when life feels downright impossible and you don't see a way out of a situation, if God wants to bless you, it won't be reliant on you impressing another human being, it will be reliant on His plan for you, and not a single hurricane that Satan can send your way can stop it. So don't let your reliance on what you think others think about you control the gauge of your joy. *Living out your days trying to impress or prove yourself to another human being is one of the fastest ways to find yourself in a state of depression and overwhelm. If we want to live joyfully and freely, we have to just be ourselves and stop thinking we have to play the part.*

Just a few weeks ago I was reminded of this more than ever when I was asked to do my first national talk with a company I greatly admire and respect. It was a huge honor and a dream to be asked to speak nationally and I just felt it in my bones that God had a reason for this opportunity falling on my lap. I knew He was going to use it to better His kingdom and that there was someone out there who needed to hear the encouraging words I knew God would speak through me. Now, though I may have appeared confident to others around me, I inwardly honestly thought, "Will they like what I am going to say and how I speak? Will I stutter my words or mess up? Will I be able to prove myself to this company and my audience as a professional and as a knowledgeable nutritionist?"

For two months day in and day out, I worked on this speech and presentation, which would break down my ten healthy lifestyle principles found in my first book *Live Healthy With Laura.* I designed a beautiful PowerPoint and worked on memorizing my forty-five minute script every single day. I recited what I was going to say in the shower, on the road, and then silently in my head each night before I went to sleep. This was going to be the biggest event in my career and I was determined to do an amazing job and impress the pants off of those who gave me this opportunity to speak. I had spoken in many rooms full of people before, but nationwide and on camera? Yeah, this was a bit more pressure than I was used to.

I kept telling my mom, "I just hope I do a good job." And she kept reminding me, "Laura, God didn't bring this opportunity to you by mistake. You don't have to do anything but show up and just try your best. God will handle the rest." Through her constant encouragement it reminded me of the fact that really, I had nothing to prove. I just had to do my best and be myself. So, as I do before any talk, I went to bed early so I would feel rested the next day. Then, the next day came and I woke up with energy and excitement. I was ready to kill this talk!

When the time finally came, I got dressed in my sleek black business suit and made my way to the studio. Before I knew it, I was on camera giving my talk and the talk that I had been practicing for two whole months. It was going beautifully until I was interrupted by the marketing manager letting me know that the viewers were saying the sound was off and no one could make out a single word I said! I was mortified, but, as directed, I proceeded to start over again. A few minutes into my second attempt to deliver my speech, I was stopped for the same issue, and then a few minutes later it was decided that the whole event would just need to be postponed. I was disappointed but at least I felt that I had wholeheartedly given it my all and I knew that the next time I came back I would be on my game once more.

Two weeks later and the night before my rescheduled talk, there was a knock on my bedroom door at 1 a.m. It was my seven-year-old daughter who said, "Mommy, my tummy hurts." Within seconds of me opening my bedroom door, I looked down and vomit was covering the floor. It all happened so quickly, and I instantly realized, "Oh no! We've been hit with a stomach virus!" I couldn't believe it. The very night before my talk, we had been hit with a stomach virus that had not graced our home in over two years! What are the odds, right? It was about halfway through the night when I found myself once again getting out of bed to clean up vomit when my husband said, "Jeez, Laura, I don't know what you did to the devil but he does not like you!" He wasn't trying to discourage me but instead he was making an observation. I mean, of course, the night before this big talk everything would ironically go south! At that point I just laughed to keep from crying because really, he was right. God had a plan to use me the next day and Satan was going to throw every single dart my way he could in an attempt to keep me from showing up.

A few hours later, around ten o'clock the next morning, the stomach bug hit me and it hit me hard. I was taking anti-nausea medicine and dropping peppermint oil on my tongue around the clock just trying my hardest not to vomit (because we all know that once it starts, it doesn't stop). I just kept thinking "I just can't do this! I am anything BUT on my game today! I feel like death." It honestly was like a bad nightmare straight from hell that I couldn't escape and that just wouldn't end. I knew I had to show up for this talk, but I felt depression sink in because I no longer felt confident that I could prove myself to this company or effectively reach my audience. I was barely hanging on by a thread that day, and so all that was left to do was pray. So I did. I prayed hard and I had other close friends and family praying for me as well.

That night, somehow, God gave me the strength to kill that dang talk. I didn't have it in me to do anything but show up and just try my best, so that's what I did. I felt sick to my stomach but God showed up and gave me more than enough energy to get through. Twenty minutes before I was scheduled to begin speaking, my nausea completely lifted and I felt revitalized. It truly was a miracle! That night when I was speaking, I felt God speak to my heart and tell me to stop looking to others for approval but only to look to Him. So I did. I stopped worrying about who was watching me and what they thought, and I just spoke from my heart and gave my all. As a result, God lifted my spirit in such an amazing way! And though I knew that my circumstances were anything but ideal, I also knew that I was offering the Lord my best and He was pleased with me, and that knowledge in itself gave me all the joy in the world.

I really and truly want that same joy for you too as you go about your life. Therefore, I am urging you to please stop. Please stop trying to live for the approval of your boss, your friend, your spouse, or your audience. Live to please and perform for God, and God alone. Just show up and do the best you can every day without fear of the rejection of others. *Pray for God to shift your perspective and focus on Him, and Him alone, and know that by doing this, you will be gifted with this very same indescribable peace and joy that will ultimately become your strength.*

DIVE DEEP:

- Do you ever feel the need to measure up in any way?

- Do you fear rejection and ridicule from others?

- Pray today that God will help you shift your focus to pleasing Him and Him alone.

Broken, But Not Destroyed

"I can do all things through Christ
who gives me strength!"
—Philippians 4:13

I am writing this book in real time and I just feel the need to report that man, it has been a *week*. Or maybe more accurately, I should say, it has been more like a month of what has seemed to be a wave of trial after trial that seems to be desperately trying to drown my family. From my mom's newfound diagnosis with breast cancer, to my little sister who was nearly on death's doorstep with double pneumonia COVID, to my husband who was almost out of a job for simply standing up for what he believes in, to my first national talk going south when my microphone stopped working, to getting our car keyed yesterday, I can honestly admit to you that my spirit truly feels broken and my happy-go-lucky mood? Yeah, that has been squashed this week as well. When it rains, it sure pours and my goodness, am I drenched! Truthfully, yesterday after I received the picture from my husband of our newest vehicle all keyed up, I just wanted to look up to the sky and shout, "Why God, why?!"

Now, hear me out. I want you to know that I absolutely am not saying that I think God is some mean kid with a magnifying glass staring down on an ant hill. But I also *do* know that we live in a fallen world and sometimes bad things will just happen, and we won't always be able to make sense of it and, frankly, we may feel a little angry about our circumstances. I am sure at some point in your life you, too, have also felt the sting and repercussions of Eve taking that first bite of that apple. Sometimes, it just seems to be one thing after the next and it's just enough to break our spirit. It's hard to understand why God allows bad things to happen. It's easy to think, "Why me? Why my family?" We want to know why us and when on God's green earth are we going to catch a break?

Unfortunately, life just has a funny way of knocking us down on our butts sometimes. But, God. He knows us well and He knows what we can handle, and He has a reason for allowing everything that takes place in our lives to happen. You see, *as ironic as it may sound, I am a firm believer that we can't reach our full joy potential if everything in life is always smooth sailing. Bumps in the road can in fact be a blessing.*

As much as we wish everything would always go according to our plans and we wouldn't hit bumps in the road, I believe that at times we are supposed to hit these bumps so that we can really practice walking by faith alone. Is anything better for a little perspective refresher than hitting rock bottom? I think not. I don't know about you, but times like these sure make me appreciate what many would label as a "boring," non-eventful day! Now am I saying that I have enjoyed these last few weeks? I sure as heck have not. That being said, deep down I know that God is faithful and loving and He has a reason for every trial me or my family is asked to endure, and I know the light is coming. The truth is my spirit has felt very broken over these last few weeks. I haven't been the vivacious light I want to be for others around me because my discouraged heart has shone through. But that is okay because no one expects me to always be on my game, and the same goes for you. But with God, I know He will carry me through whatever trials occur in my life and I know that He will always come through and show me the light once again. My spirit has been broken, yes, and I know this full and well, but I also know that with God, He will never let me be destroyed! Yes, I will be tested. Yes, I will get discouraged. And yes, I will get overwhelmed with life at times. But I know that if I choose to walk by faith, call on Him daily, and not pretend that I have the strength to walk alone, He will always carry me and my family through and we will not be shaken.

But let me just go ahead and warn you now. When we are stuck in hard times like these that just seem to constantly be hailing down on us, Satan knows that we are vulnerable and it's not a matter of *if* but *when* he will try to convince us that we have been destroyed. He wants us to think that life is never going to get better. He wants us to think that our trials are our new normal and that there is no way out. But we can't listen to him! Think about Jesus for a moment. In chapter 4 in the book of Matthew, it is written that for forty days Jesus fasted in the desert. I can't even begin to imagine how hungry, thirsty, and exhausted he was, can you? In human terms, I imagine that He was "just over it." Satan was tempting him around the clock to give in to eating and to give up and give in. But He didn't. I can only imagine how broken His human form felt. But Jesus refused to be broken by the enemy. He pressed through and He made it out of that desert without ever once throwing in the towel.

Now, many look at this passage and assume it is just a lesson on temptation, but I think it is also a beautiful example of how God wants us to press through life's trials and never believe the enemy's lie that "this is it" because, hear me out, it's not! Jesus made it through and with Him, so can we. We may feel broken, exhausted, and worn thin by our life's circumstances, but we are not broken, my friend! The enemy does not really have the power to destroy us because with Christ we can conquer all! So, when He is busy whispering lies into your ear, how about you whisper one back: "Hey Satan! Guess what? I can endure ALL things with Christ who gives me His strength! So back off because I will press on until I reach the other side of this hurdle, whether you like it or not! So, don't even bother trying to feed me anymore of your lies because I won't be listening!" Say these words out loud, believe them in your heart, and then show the devil what's up. Stand strong and show him how powerful you are with God on your side. Then, stay tuned and be on the lookout, because I promise you that a breakthrough is on the horizon!

DIVE DEEP:

- Do you have faith that after each storm a rainbow is coming and that God has a reason for allowing each trial in your life to take place?

- When life knocks you down do you stay there or do you get back up?

- Is prayer your first or last resort when troubles hit?

Journaling For a More Joyful Soul

"Preserve your memories, keep them well, what
you forget you can never retell."
7—Louisa May Alcott

Sometimes life can feel like such a blur and because of how quickly it goes, I find it easy to forget all the good God has done in the past. Days turn into weeks and months turn into years and before we know it, a decade has gone by. And though we wish that life would stand still, it just doesn't. Now unfortunately, we have no power over the rapid speed of life, how swiftly our kids grow up, or how quickly we age. But one thing we *can* do is to write each chapter of our lives down on paper so that we never forget.

Sometimes life throws a situation at us that feels so daunting that at the time, it may feel like we will never recover. We may see no way around the roadblock in front of us and because we feel insecure in our circumstances, our spirit can easily get discouraged and we can often lose hope. During these times, though, we have a choice. We can either wallow in our fear and our discontentment or we can stop and take the time to look back and remember all God has done for us in the past. When we stop to do this, we can once again be encouraged and reminded that He has never left us stranded and He isn't about to start now.

For me, journaling is how I keep myself from forgetting all of the hardships that God has walked me through in the past and it's actually something I have made a point to do for years. I wish I could say I journal daily or weekly but honestly it's more like monthly during this crazy, busy period of my life. However, I make sure that when I do journal, I go into detail about each aspect of my life. I write down how I am feeling, the thoughts I'm having over each situation, and what I am praying and hoping will change or be resolved. Then, I make a point to go back and read last month's journal entry and without fail, I am always reminded of God's faithfulness. I quickly discover that most of the time, whatever I was feeling last month, as difficult and hopeless as it seemed then, feels miniscule or forgotten in the present month and I get to see and write down how God came through.

Because I have made it a point to journal for so long, I can pull out one of my old journals and reread and relive the thoughts and fears I was experiencing during our financial struggles, our marriage struggles, our fertility struggles, and throughout my struggle with anxiety and depression. Reading through my old journals brings me right back. Instantly, when I read those words that I wrote years prior, I remember the fear and anxiety I felt during those times. I remember how helpless my situation seemed and I remember how I cried out to God for help in my time of need.

Here are a few excerpts from my journal over the years:

- In the midst of our infertility journey and after suffering a couple miscarriages I wrote:

  "We are still waiting and trusting God for a baby but I am starting to worry it may never happen."

  I am now the mama of a beautiful seven-year-old little girl and a precious blonde haired, blue-eyed four-year-old little boy.

- Shortly after my daughter was born and we were at the very beginning stages of building and investing in our company I wrote:

  "Both of our accounts are currently over drafted and we are anxiously waiting for checks to come in."

  Our company just had its most profitable year yet.

- Seven years after I was hit with anxiety and depression I wrote:

  "Will I ever be free of this anxiety and depression and experience true joy again?"

Though I still have my occasional "off days," I can happily report that I am no longer suffering with my mental health as I once was and I now feel free.

By reading back through my journals it becomes evident once again that God has always been by my side (and I know He is by yours, too). And though my prayers have not always been answered in my preferred timeframe, I can always look back and see that He did answer each one of them. Also, by reading through my journal, I can make more sense of the "yeses" the "noes" and the "not now's." Sometimes, I even look back and thank God that He gave me a different answer than the one I was hoping for.

So yes, life can get sticky and sometimes just downright hard. *But if we hold onto the knowledge of what God has done for us in the past, it gives us hope and strength to press on in the present and into the future.* And what better way to remember what God has brought us through than to journal often? What better way to remember all He has done than to go back and read through old trials and hardships that He has carried us through? In 1 Peter 5:7 it says to "give all of your worries and cares to God, for He cares about what happens to you." So let's stop trying to process life's challenges on our own and give them to God, shall we?

This year I challenge you to do just that. Pray often and give your cares to God as the Bible instructs us to. But I also challenge you to start keeping a journal as well (if you don't already). And although there is no miraculous power behind journaling itself, I can attest that there *is* great power in reminding oneself often of all the good God has done when life's circumstances breed discouragement. This world we live in, it's a hard place, but just think about how much more joyful and less anxious we all would be if we had a little extra reminder of God's faithfulness! So, why wait? Why not pick out that cute and colorful journal (mine is currently hot pink and teal) and start writing your story today? I have a feeling it's going to play out to be a good one.

DIVE DEEP:

- Do you keep a journal and if so how often do you write in it?

- Pinpoint three ways that God has come through for you in this last year (and if you haven't already, write them down).

- Do you truly have faith that God will continue to guide and care for you in this coming year? If you have any doubt, go back and reread your answer to the last bullet point.

Embracing Your Senses to Reignite Your Soul

*"But blessed are your eyes because they see, and
your ears because they hear."*
—Matthew 13:16

The beginning of this chapter may appear to be dripping with cheese but nevertheless, do me a favor and just try to run with it, okay? Let's start with a few questions. When was the last time you actually stopped to smell the roses? No, like I mean really. How long ago was it? When was the last time you actually stopped to stargaze or bask in the beauty of a sunrise or a sunset? When was the last time you ate something so out-of-this-world amazing that you closed your eyes just so you could fully take in all of the flavors and textures? When was the last time you felt something with your hands that felt softer than butter, so you kept holding on? And lastly, when was the last time you heard something so beautiful that it stopped you in your tracks?

Do you want to know why I think so many of us adults find life so dull and void of excitement? It's because they aren't embracing all the amazing senses God has given them! Maybe it's because they are too busy to notice or maybe they have just gotten so tied up in "adulting" that they have forgotten what it was like to just take a pause and stare up into a cotton candy sky or watch the waves crash onto the shore, smell a vanilla scented candle, eat dark chocolate slowly, listen to the birds sing or children laughing, run their fingers through a horses mane, or feel the unique fuzziness of a caterpillar their toddler brought them.

My friend, there is beauty all around you! You just have to take a pause to notice and be willing to open your eyes to see. But I get it. Sometimes we just get so caught up in going from one thing to the next that life becomes a hazy. We try our very best to hurry up in an attempt to slow down but it never really happens. I felt like this for years. But one day, I decided to commit an hour every Sunday after church to baking or cooking. As quickly as I can, I come home to kick off my shoes, change into some comfy clothes, turn on some Ed Sheeran tunes ,and get to work.

Okay, so I like to be in the kitchen but what does this have to do with the five senses? Well, everything! Cooking and baking for me have not only helped me slow down, they also have helped me tune into the smell, sight, texture, taste, and yes, even the sounds of foods as they cook or cool on the stove top. I am by no means a chef or professional baker, but the reason I have had success in coming up with so many yummy recipes (that you can see featured in my first book or on my blog if you're interested), is because I have used these senses that God gave me!

What colors do I like to see? What smells do I enjoy? What textures of foods and baked goods are my favorite? What flavors do I love to taste the most and what sounds in the kitchen bring comfort to my soul? Truly, being in the kitchen brings me such joy because again, it has taught me to disconnect from the chaotic world surrounding me and just be still. It has taught me to ultimately "stop and smell the roses" in other areas of life as well and it has taught me to take the time to soak up the beauty around me.

Have you ever smelled, heard, tasted, seen, or felt something that instantly brought back a joyous memory from your childhood? For me, it's hearing a lawn mower and smelling that fresh cut grass. It brings me back to warm summer days where I would be playing with my siblings in the backyard and my dad would be cutting the grass nearby. Those days bring back feelings of excitement, contentment, and joy. Nowadays, when I step outside and the grass is being mowed, I take a second to really listen and to breathe in that smell of that fresh cut grass that I love so much. I call little unexpected warm moments like this "hugs from God."

Growing up, I was a happy, carefree child and I have lots of memories of my mom in the kitchen as well. The memories I have with her include various comforting smells, tastes, textures, colors, and sounds.

When I became a mom, I decided that I too wanted to paint the same memories for my children. So, from the time that my daughter was born seven years ago, I was determined to spend more time in the kitchen with my kids. These days, I try my best to include them whenever I can when I'm baking and cooking and I just love the memories we have made so far.

But really, for ten years now I have been what I like to call "playing" in the kitchen. Again, the kitchen is a place where I feel that God has allowed me to discover a peace and unique joy, and it has been a place that God used to spark my passion in nutrition and lead me to where I am today. In fact, despite my struggle with depression, even when I was at my worst, I still spent time in the kitchen. My company and blog *Live Healthy With Laura* were ultimately born as a result of many Sunday afternoons spent using my senses in the kitchen. It was born as a result of me choosing to slow down enough to hear God's voice. Because really, if we are always caught up in the chaos of life, how are we going to hear Him? How are we going to discover hobbies and activities that bring us joy? We can't.

So, what about you? What is an activity that you could implement into your weekly routine that you think could help you slow down and tune into your senses and bring you more joy? Maybe start with asking yourself what comforting, joyful memory as a child you want to recreate for yourself or your family. Maybe ask yourself to reminisce and think back to the things that used to bring you joy as a child that maybe you have forgotten about. What sounds, colors, tastes, or textures do you or did you enjoy and which ones bring you back to the good old days?

Listen, you don't have to love being in the kitchen as I do (or you might, you just may not know it yet) but you can try something else! If you are really feeling clueless about where to start then go for a hike in God's green earth and stop to smell that fresh, clean, and crisp air. Pick up different leaves and flowers along the way and feel them with your fingers and breathe in their scent. Pick up sewing, painting, tennis, kayaking, golfing, or whatever sparks your interest and then put away your phone, let go of the world around you, and really soak it all in. And even if you are in a season right now that you strongly feel that there is not a single extra moment to pursue or start something new, I challenge you to search and find beauty within your day. Because I promise you it's there. *Slow down enough to tune into your five God-given senses wherever you are and whatever you are doing, and then get ready to feel your joy increase and your soul be revived!*

DIVE DEEP:

- Do you tune into your five senses often and allow them to bring you joy?

- What past time centers you the most and allows you to use your senses?

- Take a minute today to thank God for your senses and make it a point to honor him by intentionally using each of them today.

Quieting The Noise to Hear God's Voice

"Be still and know that I am God."
—Psalm 46:10

Chaos is just our everyday reality in the world we live in, isn't it? Traffic noise, music blasting, notification chimes going off on our phone, kids fussing, and well, you get it. Life is oftentimes anything but quiet. One thing I have found, though, is that when I feel my joy is lacking, one of the first things I start to pay more attention to is the amount of noise in my life. Now, I don't just mean audible noise that you and I can actually hear, but anything that causes chaos within our minds. Even though I am a pretty regimented person and I restrict myself in regards to social media, as you now well know, I still sometimes lose my peace and once I do, my joy instantly goes out the window. When this occurs, I will often find myself getting irritable because I feel that I don't have a moment to even comprehend the joys in my life surrounding me because I am stuck in a sea of noise and chaos. It's exhausting and it can be downright depressing if you ask me.

This happened to me a couple months back when the holidays were quickly approaching. I got this sinking feeling one day that something internally just wasn't right. I felt as if my head was stuck in pure chaos mode. My phone was ringing off the hook and I felt as if I was always speaking to someone, if not in person at work, then on the phone. To-do lists were running through my head as I laid down each night, my house was a mess, laundry was backed up, and it just seemed that we were constantly in the car and on the go to yet another festive event. My life was lacking peace and the silence I needed to really take time to speak to God and then hear His voice. My morning routine went out the window and ultimately, because I was not making the time to talk to God, I also started lacking in that "peace that surpasses all understanding" as well. On top of that, I noticed that my anxiety started creeping in again, so needless to say, I knew that something had to give.

So, what did I do? I put myself on phone restriction and essentially grounded myself for a few days. I put my phone on do not disturb for about eight hours straight each day and I said "no" to everything I possibly could so that my family and I could rediscover that joy that ultimately comes with peace. I carved out time for things that fulfilled me and my family like gingerbread house decorating, watching the original Rudolph movie, and wrapping presents with the kids. I also unapologetically looked for windows of time that I could spend time *alone* just so I could regroup and hear myself think again. (Anyone else in the ambivert club? If you are, you know that time alone really isn't optional if you want to recharge.) I would take an Epsom bath or hide away to take a cat nap before the afternoon school run. I also tried my very best to get to bed earlier and stop burning the candle at both ends so I could wake up earlier and start my day talking to God.

I don't know about you, but the older I get the more difficult and chaotic life seems to be. If I go day after day not speaking to God because I am in over my head, I almost instantly lose my peace. Even if things are going smoothly and nothing really seems "wrong," if my perspective on life gets skewed and I stop talking to God, those feelings of hopelessness and overwhelm creep in. But if I ask God, He always centers me. He guides me and helps me find glimpses of joy in the midst of all the hustle and bustle. But I can't just sit back and expect Him to do everything. It is up to *me* to make and take the time to consistently speak to Him and read His word. Our circumstances in life will always be waxing and waning, but God is ever present in our lives and He is waiting to grant us that joy and peace that the world can't give us.

Embracing the quiet and making room and time to be alone with God will never fail to restore your joy. This chaotic world we live in aside from social media distracts us, but we don't have to let it. So, my advice is that you practice saying yes, but also practice saying no so that you don't miss out on the joy that peace and quiet can bring you. Only when we make room for silence can we really start to recognize the blessings in our life.

However, keep in mind that the culture and world we live in will not support you. It, and society as a whole, will always make it seem acceptable and normal to live in chaos. So it is up to us to stand strong and break away from society norms and make room for quiet in our lives. Life has taught me that keeping up with the Joneses and checking every box is oftentimes quite overrated. Always feeling the need to be logged on (as we have previously discussed) is overrated. Saying "yes" to every social event is overrated and spending time in peace and quiet with God is underrated. So, if you feel yourself lacking peace and joy in your life today, I challenge you to think back to the last time you had a moment of silence in your life and time with just yourself and God. If you realize that it has been a hot minute, then I challenge you to make some changes in your life and introduce quiet once again starting *today.*

DIVE DEEP:

- Do you start your day by talking to God or by checking your phone?

- Do you lack peace in your life? If so, can you pinpoint what is stealing it?

- Do you make room for quiet in your life daily? If not, what can you do to change that?

But, What If?

"For God has not given us a spirit of fear, but of power and of love and of a sound mind."
—2 Timothy 1:7

I sat in my car staring at that three-story brick building, wishing I didn't have to go inside. I called my sister to chat, I checked my email, I twiddled my thumbs, and then I couldn't procrastinate any longer. It was time to go inside and find out if what I was hoping was a cyst in my breast was really just a cyst. Flash back to over the summer, my mom was diagnosed with aggressive breast cancer and I was told that due to the gene mutation she tested positive for, my chances for developing breast cancer were in the higher range. So, I didn't have a choice but to go get this "cyst" checked out.

Anyone who knows me well or who has read my last book knows that it is no secret that I struggle in medical situations and I always have. I grew up with both parents in the medical field and I know all too well the reality of a grim medical diagnosis and how much it can alter one's life. I also struggled to stay pregnant for years, so I suffer with PTSD trauma and I get triggered nearly every time I walk into a doctor's office or a hospital (yes, even though I am on medication and it's not nearly as bad as it once was, I am still triggered and it sucks). Waiting for a doctor to come in and give me test results is hell for me. We all have triggers and though others may not be able to relate, waiting for test results and being in the thick of medical situations is mine. Thankfully though, I have learned some very powerful tactics that have helped me cope in the waiting period.

Before I move on to what I have learned to do when fear is attempting to paralyze me, let me ask you this. Has the thought ever crossed your mind *"things are so good right now that I just know something is about to go wrong?"* If so, know that you are not alone. I unfortunately have had the devil whisper those triggering words into my ear more times than I count.

Fear downright drains the life out of you, does it not? Everything might be going smoothly around us but instead of being able to process the beauty and joyful blessings in our lives, we are driven by fear and focus on those two frightening little words: *"What if?"* The ironic thing about fear though is how much energy it steals from us but how rarely those fears actually become a reality.

Remember how we talked about the importance of journaling? Well, interestingly enough, when I read back through my various entries from years past I discover that most of the things I spent time worrying about never actually have come into play, which then reminds me of the cold hard truth: *fear of tomorrow steals the joy from the here and now and makes me miss out on life in a big way.*

I want to live freely and without the chains of fear gripping my every waking moment, don't you? The question is *how* do we do this? How do we achieve this when we don't know what those test results are going to read and we don't know tomorrow holds? I wish I could tell you that I have mastered the art of going through life without the fear of "what if" but the truth is, I still struggle. Yet, one thing I have learned is to tell myself what I *do* know in the midst of the unknown and that is that fear does not come from God, not even a little bit and not ever. Instead, it is Satan's attempt to distract us from all the blessings in our life and all that God has for us to do. The enemy knows how much worry and fear bleed us dry. He is good at planting little seeds of fear in our minds to handicap us and leave us feeling stuck so that we no longer have the willpower to keep going.

So, what have I learned to do? *I tell the devil to shut up, back off and go away.* Yes, I seriously speak those exact words sometimes silently and sometimes out loud. And then I ask God to speak His truth to me and help restore my peace. I also flip to my Bible app and read through verse after verse about anxiety until I feel the enemy flee. Then, I try to change my inner dialogue and thoughts of the situation. Instead of thinking, "What if this is it? What if I am about to get horrible, life altering news?" Or "What if this situation, this opportunity, or this pregnancy doesn't work out?" I start thinking, *"But what if it does?"* What if these test results prove to be just fine? What if this opportunity or this pregnancy does, in fact, work out beautifully?" I also start to remind myself that even if it doesn't, God has never abandoned me, and He will walk me through each trial as He always has and I *will* be okay.

The other day while I was sitting on that exam table waiting for the radiologist to come in I decided to silence the "what ifs" and instead pray. I prayed for the Lord's strength to hear whatever news the doctor had for me—good or bad. I said, "God, I know you have plans to prosper me and not to harm me. Please settle my spirit and help calm my fears." And though I can't say I felt instantly relaxed and at ease, I did feel a peace knowing that God loves me and He wrote my story long ago. Whatever news I was going to be given was supposed to be part of my story and so it was up to me to either embrace and accept it or fight it. So, I prayed with open hands as I did years ago when I was struggling with infertility. Whatever was supposed to come into play in my life would come into play, and regardless of which way the tables turned, I knew God had my back.

After about fifteen minutes (that seemed like an hour) of waiting alone in that exam room, the doctor finally walked in. "Everything looks just fine, Laura. That cyst looks benign and of no concern. We will see you in a year!" she said. And just like that, my mind was put at ease and the days I had spent worrying about all the "what ifs" had been forgotten. But I didn't just move on. Instead, I took a few minutes on the drive home to first, of course, thank God for my positive results but also to remind myself that *even if* my fears had played out, God would have carried me through as He always has. God has my back, and He has yours when fear and doubt hit and He knows what we can handle. Trials in life will inevitably come and good news is not always promised, but regardless of what life throws our way, we can have peace if only we can trust Him. We have a choice in this life to stay frozen in our fear and let it eat away at our joy or to speak truth in the face of fear. *We must honor God by remembering that even if our "what ifs" become our reality, we can rest easy and confidently knowing that He will see us to the other side.*

DIVE DEEP:

- Are you currently being paralyzed by the fear of "what if"?

- Do you trust God to carry you through even if your "what ifs" become your reality?

- Talk to God and lay your fears at His feet today and then remind yourself who fear really comes from (Hint: It's not from God.)

No Thanks, I'll Pass

"The right thing to do and the hard thing to do are usually the same."
—Steve Maraboli

"Please, God, send someone else," Moses said to God. Moses was being told by God to go do the hard thing and confront Pharaoh and ask him to free his people. But yet, Moses knew this task was going to be difficult and force him out of his comfort zone, so he chose the "no thanks, I'll pass" quick response to deflect the responsibility and the challenge that was being placed on him.

How often have you felt this way and said these words? How often have you skidded your heels and done everything you possibly could to avoid being pushed outside of your comfort zone? Honestly, for me it's been more times than I can count. I'll just come out and say it. I love predictability and I hate, hate, hate change with a passion. But change is how we grow, is it not? Challenges that require us or our lives to change stretch us. However, they also typically end up blessing us abundantly as well. But how often do we try to run from the hard thing, the hard choice, or the change that we know needs to be made just to stay in our comfortable little bubble? The answer is that statistically, it happens a lot. But the million dollar question is, *by settling for a comfortable life and resisting change, what joys and blessings are we missing out on?* Spoiler alert—we are missing out on a lot.

My pastor recently reminded our church that God doesn't want us to remain the old 2021 version of ourselves. Instead, he wants us to embrace change and growth even if it is uncomfortable in the beginning. God wants us to embrace the new and improved 2022 version of us (and yes, even if others don't understand or like it). Only then can we experience that "full life" that is talked about in the book of John and can we experience that God-given joy that isn't depicted by our day-to-day circumstances. But to do that, we have to remember that *resisting change, as uncomfortable in the beginning as it may be, can ultimately keep us from experiencing our best, most joy-filled life.* If we feel a pull on our hearts to take a leap of faith and confront someone, switch jobs, write that book, or relocate to serve others in some way, it is up to us to be obedient.

If life has felt dull and void of excitement lately, then I want you to consider the off-chance that maybe you are stuck in your security bubble and not taking a step you know in your heart you need to take. Think back to the story of Moses. He resisted God a total of five times and gave God five different excuses as to why he wanted to comfortably stay planted where he was. It wasn't until He finally obeyed and chose to do the hard thing by bravely going to Pharaoh that God chose to bless him for his obedience by entrusting Him with more authority and power. Also, let's not forget that because Moses obeyed God, thousands of people were freed from slavery!

You may be thinking, "Okay, but what does the story of Moses have to do with me?" Well, it has a lot to do with you and I because Moses's story is a reminder that by holding back and resisting what God has for us to do, we and many others may be missing out on groundbreaking moments and blessings that we cannot even begin to imagine.

Have you ever considered that maybe it's not that your glass is empty at all? Maybe it's the fact that you keep drinking out of the same glass and are afraid of change? In Deuteronomy 28:1–2 it says, "Now it shall be, if you diligently obey the Lord your God, being careful to do all His commandments which I command you today, the Lord your God will set you high above all the nations of the earth. All these blessings will come upon you and overtake you if you obey the Lord your God." So again, with change can ultimately come blessings and opportunities that we could never begin to fathom. But in order to experience any of these, it's up to us to do the work and stop resisting the change.

I am not going to beat around the bush. With change often comes hardship. God doesn't promise us that choosing to obey Him and embracing change in any area of our lives will ever be easy or comfortable. But he *does* promise us that with obedience comes blessings and these blessings will always be accompanied by a more joyful spirit. So how can we really experience that God-given joy if we choose to stay planted where we are and refuse to grow? We can't. So, my friend, my message to you is this: *stop viewing a change as a curse and instead, choose to recognize it for what it is—an opportunity to grow and to be blessed.*

DIVE DEEP:

- Do you typically resist change or do you welcome it?

- In what area of your life are you dragging your feet and telling God "no thanks, I'll pass" like Moses?

- Are you ready to get unstuck and pursue all that God has for you to do?

Taking Charge of Your Inner Voice

"Watch what you tell yourself.
You're likely to believe it."
—Russ Kyle

I once had a middle school boyfriend break up with me but first felt the need to tell me, "There's just nothing special about you." That was almost twenty years ago and I still remember that day. I still remember how this young, immature middle school boy made me, a young, vulnerable thirteen-year-old girl, feel. I had just gotten over a very awkward acne prone skin, back brace wearing stage and I finally was building my confidence. That is, until he knocked me down with his cruel words.

I honestly carried his words with me for a long time after that. In fact, in high school I never got asked out, not even once until I later met my husband. I remember how I would hear his words repeat inside my head, and there were days I believed them to be true. "Is something wrong with me? Is there really nothing about me that is special or that stands out?" I asked myself these questions over and over and I found myself searching for an answer for a very long time.

Words hurt. Words spoken by others and words spoken from within ourselves can be crushing, debilitating, and can absolutely steal our joy. We grow up hearing that "sticks and stones may break my bones but words will never hurt me." Yet, that couldn't be further from the truth. Unfortunately, we can't control the words that come out of the mouths of others but one thing we *can* control are the words we speak to others and the words we speak to ourselves. Once we learn to speak to ourselves in an uplifting, encouraging, and loving way our whole life and perspective have the opportunity to completely change; but it takes practice. One way to evaluate our words and our inner voice is to do a little self-reflection. Start by asking yourself a few questions, such as:

> Do you speak to yourself in the same way that you would to a child or a friend?
>
> Do the words you say reflect Christ and do they spread positivity and joy, or are they negative and degrading?
>
> When you look in the mirror, what type of person do you see staring back at you?
>
> • Do you believe you are treasured and deserve a full, joy-filled life?

Are you being anchored by chains and feelings of unworthiness that the world or someone bestowed upon you in the past?

What we believe about ourselves to be true can either make us or break us, ground us or shake us. You and I are treasured in the eyes of God and we must remember that if and when the world makes us feel otherwise. Confidence from the Lord increases our joy from within and is contagious to others around us, and it's not dependent on the words spoken by another human being, including ourselves. If we want a glass half full approach, we have to start by looking within ourselves, evaluating our inner dialogue, and asking ourselves if it reflects what God says about us.

We have to remember that *the way we view ourselves is just as significant as the way we view our lives and the world around us. If we want to experience joy in our lives and make a difference in this world, we have to first believe we are worthy and treasured in the eyes of God.* We have to stop believing the lie that we are unworthy or not special or treasured because that is a lie from the pit of hell. God tells us in the Bible that we are "fearfully and wonderfully made," but what I want to know is *do you really believe that?*

For years, I had the worst self-esteem that, as you can imagine, my middle school years had something to do with. But one thing I have yet to dive into is how a few years prior, at the age of nine, I developed cystic acne that left deep scars all over my face. Then later, at the age of twelve, I was diagnosed with severe scoliosis that required an immediate, extensive, nine-hour operation that placed me in a back brace for an entire year thereafter. I had just finally let my tomboy years go and was starting to become increasingly aware and conscious of my outward appearance when I was left in a body cast from the waist up.

I remember how my mom and I would search for hours for shirts that would hide my brace and I remember all too clearly how my fun-loving brothers would think it was hilarious to knock on me like I was a door whenever I walked by. I remember spending thirty minutes every morning trying to cover up each scar on my face with concealer and I remember how much I dreaded leaving the house. Yes, my middle school years were, without a doubt, a hellish experience but I don't tell you all of this to gain pity. Instead, I want to tell you about how God used a time in my life to teach me how to lean on Him and speak confidence and love back into myself. This didn't happen overnight and it did take practice, but eventually I learned my self-worth and I chose to really believe it. I wish I could say that it was after those awkward middle school years that I recovered and instantly gained this "God confidence" that I've been speaking about but unfortunately that wasn't the case.

Throughout my twenties I was no longer plagued by acne or a back brace but was then hit with a mental health struggle that I wasn't prepared for and that left me feeling alone and ashamed. I then spent years putting in more work to not only heal my mental health, but also to truly believe that my mental illness did not define me.

God told me I was treasured and special and that my life had a purpose. So I prayed for His supernatural strength day after day to believe it.

From the outside looking in, I can't argue that my life has appeared pretty easy sailing. But let me tell you, I have had my share of struggles and I am sure you have as well. Life hasn't been easy but I know my struggles were not without purpose. God used them for His glory and for a purpose, and now today, at the age of thirty-two, I can happily report that I am a woman of confidence who knows wholeheartedly that she is worthy. And because I now know this and make it a point to breathe words of love and life back into myself daily, I can encourage others in a way I never would have been able to before. Of course, I still have days that I struggle because well, I am human and still prone to moments of self-consciousness but thankfully, this is not an everyday battle I face anymore.

Have you ever heard that saying, "Empowered women empower women"? Do you know what it really means to be "empowered"? First let's just go ahead and change that up a bit and say that in a broader sense of "Empowered people empower people." Because in all actuality, this applies to everyone. But to me, to be "empowered" means embracing the unique, beautiful, and wonderfully-made individual that you are. It means that you know you are worthy of love and respect. It means that you have a God-given confidence that shines onto others and onto the world around you. It means that you have let go of striving to "measure up" to the world's standards and you have stopped trying to be anyone other than the unique, amazing person YOU were born to be. It also means that you have placed healthy boundaries between you and anyone who tells you otherwise.

I, for one, know that implementing that last one is not always easy. But if we ask God for His help, He will give us strength to let go of the past and hurtful words within it. In Isaiah 43:18–19 He says, "Do not call to mind the former things, Or ponder things of the past. Behold, I will do something new, Now it will spring forth; Will you not be aware of it? I will even make a roadway in the wilderness, Rivers in the desert." That's right, my friend. Regardless of who or what hurt you in the past and made you feel invaluable or unloved, God is waiting to help you break free from these chains holding you back. He is waiting to do something new and exciting in your life and He is waiting to make streams in your dessert, or, in other words, He is waiting to heal your brokenness and help you regain your confidence once and for all.

In the very same way that I shared this concept in my last book *Mama, You Still Matter*, I want to reiterate once more that no one, and I repeat, no one, can breathe life into others if they are without oxygen themselves. If we want to change the world for the better and live a joy-filled life, we must remember that it starts from within us and we must never forget that the way we speak to ourselves and the things we really believe about ourselves matter.

Our self-worth isn't dependent on that number on the scale, the scars we bare on our skin or harbor from our past, our mental or physical health status, the hateful words that were once spoken to us by someone who felt the need to rip us apart, the rejection or abandonment we felt from someone we loved, that job promotion we didn't get, or whatever sly attempt the devil tries to use to make us feel less than the gem we are. Our self-worth isn't dependent on anything other than what God says about us. And what exactly does God say about us? Well, in Luke 12:7 He says, "Indeed, the very hairs of your head are all numbered. Don't be afraid; you are worth more than many sparrows." Wow, okay. So if He knows the exact number of hairs on our heads then we must be extremely valuable to Him, wouldn't you agree?

Look, I'd say that the devil has tried to steal enough from us already, so I think it's high time we stop believing his lies and commit to shutting out the hurtful voices in our head and the hurtful voices of others. Let's commit to speaking to ourselves only in a way that honors our creator and that empowers and breathes life back into our mind, body, and soul. And let's never forget that we are worthy, cherished, and deeply loved, regardless of what others think or say. Because truly we are and it is only by remembering this that we can make a difference in the lives of others and our perspective can be changed for the better.

DIVE DEEP:

- Do you speak to yourself in a way that pleases God and reflects what He says about you?

- Are you hanging onto hurtful words spoken to you from someone in your past?

- Pray today that God will help you identify the voice of the enemy and help you speak against His lies with truth.

Just Roll With It

"Go with the flow. Force nothing. Let it happen, or not happen..trusting that whichever way it goes, it's for the best."
— Mandy Hale

Have you ever caught yourself imagining and choreographing an event, holiday, or vacation coming up in your head before it even takes place? Have you ever told yourself, "This is going to be amazing!" or "We are going to have the best time!" or "We are going to make the best memories!" only to be disappointed that the event didn't meet your standards or measure up to the picture you had painted in your head? I think that many of us do this all too often because we fall into the trap of believing the highlight reel lie that *"this is how it should be."*

Having a newborn baby is "supposed" to be one of the sweetest, most magical times in your life, isn't it? Christmas time is "supposed" to be pure bliss and a family vacation at a gorgeous lake house is "supposed" to be free-sailing and chock full of candid-worthy moments. But what if life takes a turn and postpartum depression rears its ugly head and that first year of infancy isn't how you pictured it? What if you end up feeling like an anxious mess instead of relaxed and excited around the holidays, and you secretly find yourself counting down the moment until it's over? What if your toddler pukes the moment you arrive at that gorgeous lake house and you are confined to the basement, away from the rest of the family for the entire trip because you are afraid to get anyone else sick? *Is life just one big disappointment?*

Truthfully, if we play our cards right it doesn't have to be. But we have to be really careful to not fall into the trap of over-planning in our minds and dictating to ourselves how something is going to go, how something should be, and how we are supposed to feel during it. Everything I just mentioned was once my reality. I *was* that mama that was hit with postpartum depression at a time in my life that I'd told myself would be exceedingly joyful. I *was* that hot mess express a few years ago calling my doctor begging him to up my anti-anxiety medication right before Christmas. And that *was* my toddler who started to puke the moment we arrived at that serene and picture-perfect Smith Mountain Lake house a couple years back.

And truly, during those times, life did seem like one big disappointment and I felt like one, big failure because, well, I had let myself down. I would think to myself, "This wasn't at ALL how I planned it!" or "This wasn't how I was *supposed* to feel!" "Why am I miserable during a time that was *supposed* to be incredible and full of wonderful moments and memories?" "Is something wrong with me?"

As I have mentioned before, I am a dreamer and always have been. I am a hopeless romantic and I have always been a type A planner. But what I didn't realize until about the age of thirty was how much dreaming and planning was really stealing my joy. One day it hit me, and I realized I had never really let my life just flow. I had never let myself just roll with the punches and I had always put pressure on myself to try and experience something in the way that I or society or Instagram deemed as "correct."

Maybe this is foreign to you or maybe you can relate but either way, I am writing this chapter to tell you about a lesson God has taught me that I feel the need to pass on. That lesson is this: sometimes our life's experiences won't be as we imagined them to be and that's okay. Sometimes something or an event or a day we have dreamed of for a long time doesn't play out the way we thought or hoped it would, but that's okay, too. Life is beautiful but it can also be really messy. Yet, if we acknowledge this and consciously take the pressure off our shoulders to feel about or experience life in any certain way, it can be a game changer. If we just let life be as it's going to be, we actually can end up experiencing joy in some pretty unexpected places.I know I have already brought up Christmas a few chapters back but there is one specific Christmas I remember all too clearly. It was about mid-

December a couple years back when I found myself battling an unexpected wave of anxiety and depression as a result of, you guessed it, overscheduling myself. (If you read my last book *Mama, You Still Matter*, you may remember me mentioning that it is scientifically proven that overstimulation is one of the top triggers for both anxiety and depression.) Anyway, I remember just feeling numb and not in a very festive mood. I was worn thin from hosting several events in my home and felt as if I had nothing left to give to anyone, much less in contribution to the holiday spirit. But I made the decision that Christmas to just let myself have room to breathe and process the feelings I was having. Instead of pushing myself to do more, I let myself be still and feel how I was really feeling.

One sunny morning, a few days before Christmas, I decided to take my kids outside to ride bikes. It was midday and they were still in their pajamas but since I had decided that we weren't leaving the house that day, I didn't even bother telling them to get dressed. I remember sitting there on my porch steps feeling emotionally worn thin and not even having the willpower to move, when I looked up and saw my kids freely laughing and riding their bikes in circles. Within moments of watching my sweet babies having fun in their pj's and the sunlight hitting my face, I felt my spirit lifted. I felt my shoulders relax and I slowly felt my joy start to return. In fact, a few minutes later, I was playing catch with them and laughing right alongside them. It was then that I felt what I like to call a "hug from God" and I felt His peace.

You see, I had been pushing myself extra hard that Christmas and even though I knew better, every single weekend for the previous few weeks had been slam-jammed with holiday events (remember how we talked about the importance of saying "no"?). And guess what? I found myself not hardly enjoying a single one of them—yes, even "magical" Christmas light shows and "fun and festive" cookie decorating parties that were "supposed" to be enjoyable. But I didn't fight it. I knew I had overwhelmed myself and I knew from my track record that when I am overbooked, overstimulation takes over my brain and without fail, I lose my joy.

But it was on that un-orchestrated winter day on those porch steps that I felt my joy return, and I once again felt at peace. It was in that unexpected moment that I rediscovered my laughter and it was *then* that God reminded me that I am human and I am allowed to unapologetically feel how I really feel (and so can you).

If there is one thing that God has taught me throughout the years, it's this: *life is full of unexpected moments of joy that don't require a single moment of planning.* Therefore, it is up to you and I to stop dictating to ourselves how each day is supposed to go and how we are supposed to feel. It is up to us to embrace every moment of our lives and every feeling that comes with it. You and I are human and we are allowed to have good and bad days and happy and sad emotions, regardless of what glorious event or holiday is taking place.

If you want to feel less discouraged or let down in life, then I strongly encourage you to just let your perceptions of your days and experiences (whether good or bad) be as they want to be. Remind yourself that joyful moments can occur at any given time but it's not actually up to us to create them! God has already done the work of planning out each of our lives. I think it's about time that we all take a chill pill and start to really embrace the ride, don't you think?

Sometimes our days will be full of joy and wonderful, candid moments but other days, well, not so much. But that is *okay*! We aren't required to enjoy every second of every day, or every event for that matter, and we are allowed to have highs and lows. That's called life! But trust me when I tell you that if joy is your objective, there is a lot more to be found in a less orchestrated life free of so many expectations. So, why don't we stop all of the over analyzing and planning, take a deep breath and just roll with it?

DIVE DEEP:

- Do you place pressure on yourself to experience life in any certain way?

- In what areas can you better learn to relax and let life just flow?

- Think back to a time in your life that you experienced joy in an unexpected place and then thank God for that sweet memory and more like it that are sure to come.

Relationships That Breathe Life

"Pessimism is an investment in nothing.
Optimism is an investment in hope."
—Author Unknown

Who you surround yourself with *matters.* I used to not realize how much it mattered though and for years, I didn't really catch on to how much another's pessimism or optimism would impact me and my overall outlook on life. It's a known fact that you become like the company you keep, yet so often, we still expose ourselves to others that we know deep down are not good for us, do we not? Maybe it's because we have been friends for years with this person or maybe it's because this person is a family member that we can't just easily "break up" with. So we keep putting ourselves in the line of fire only to come out burned and wondering why once again, our positive outlook on life and our cheery mood have been extinguished. But isn't life hard enough on its own? As beautiful as it can be, it still can do a good job of discouraging us. Do we really need another person's pessimism weighing us down?

I am confident that if you took a moment, you could easily think of at least a person or two that you were discouraged by at some point in your life. Maybe it wasn't even anything they said to you directly, but it was just how they constantly spoke about themselves or their own lives. Maybe their "glass half empty" perspective started messing with your own perspective and you knew it. And yet, you still continued to spend time surrounding yourself with this person or these people, only to be left feeling further discouraged once again.

Maybe you went to lunch with this "friend" hoping to be encouraged about something that was weighing you down only to leave feeling more discouraged than when you arrived. Maybe they only fueled your anger towards the situation or the person you were upset at. Maybe they told you to give up on that person or that job or that dream because clearly it wasn't making you happy at the present time. (Side note: a true friend won't tell you to just give up when the going gets tough.) Or maybe they didn't hear you at all and instead spent the entire time talking about themselves and their own problems and complaining about how unhappy they were in their own lives. Instead of speaking positively and listening to you they complained about their spouse, their kids, their job, their weight, that person who cut them off on the way to lunch, or how their salad was made incorrectly.

Now before we go much further, I want to clearly state that I don't believe there is anything wrong with a good vent session once in a while. In fact, I think it can be very healthy and emotionally healing to let our emotions out and put into words how we are really feeling. I strongly believe that bottling up our emotions can do way more damage than good. *That being said, what I believe isn't healthy is when the ratio of negativity and complaining far outweigh the level of positivity and thankfulness.*I think we can all determine that we have encountered at least someone who has brought us down at one point or another. But what I really hope is that you can just as easily think of someone in your life who has left you feeling hopeful and encouraged when you were in a pit. I hope that this person met you where you were at and did not spew judgment at you for your sadness, anger, or frustration with life. I hope they made you feel safe by offering their listening ear. But I also hope they didn't let the conversation end there.

Do you remember my friend who sat with me in Panera that day as I was wallowing in my anger and sadness over not being a mother yet? Do you remember how she gave me permission to be upset but she didn't tell me everything I wanted to hear, and she didn't let me keep spiraling in my anger and pessimism? Instead, she lovingly pointed me back to God's truths and reminded me that despite my pain, He knew what was best for me and knew what He was doing. Yeah, that girl is a gem in my life and I hope you have someone like her in your life, too. Maybe this person who has come to mind has helped you through a breakup, the death of a loved one, a miscarriage, a job loss, or an illness. Maybe you even spent time with this person hoping they *would* fuel your anger, sadness, or resentment but yet, they didn't. Whoever they are, I hope you hold them close.

I am a creature of habit and as I have already expressed, I hate change with a passion. But sometimes change is not only good but also necessary if we want to better ourselves and our perspective in this life. Remember that quote that states, "You can't keep doing the same thing and expect a different result"? That quote is so incredibly true and I believe it can be applied to many areas in our lives, including relationships.

If someone has a history of being negative or dampening your spirit, more than likely they will continue to. Not to say that people can't change, but I don't think it is up to us to wait around and find out and expose ourselves to their negativity day in and day out. Now, I am not suggesting that you write these negative people a breakup letter and say "sayonara!" But what I *am* suggesting is that you really think long and hard about who you want to invest your valuable time in and who you want to expose your fragile emotions to. Because really, we are all human and none of us are resilient. If we want to stay positive and joyful in life, then we must make a conscious effort to carefully evaluate the company we keep and the circle we are in. In Proverbs 12:26 it says that "the righteous choose their friends carefully". So, in the same way that Jesus carefully selected his disciples that also became his closest friends during His time on Earth, the Bible tells us that we are to do the same.

Optimism isn't something that comes easily, especially in the world we live in, and we can't always control our surroundings or who is in our path. However, we *can* choose who we consider a "living room friend" versus a "garage or driveway friend," as my pastor puts it. We actually do get to choose which negative or positive people we allow to influence us. Positivity and thankfulness are both choices. So we have to consciously surround ourselves with friends who choose both (at least most of the time, that is) in the same way that we also have to protect ourselves from those who don't. If we want to be a light in this world, we must surround ourselves with light. Let's never forget that.

DIVE DEEP:

- Are those who you spend the most time with typically optimistic or pessimistic?

- Do your closest friends challenge you and tell you the truth, even if it isn't always what you want to hear?

- Take a few minutes today to thank God for the solid friendships in your life.

The Gift That Keeps Giving

"Each of you should use whatever gift you have received to serve others, as faithful stewards of God's grace in its various forms."
—1 Peter 4:10

It was a Tuesday and already I was ready for the week to be over. I had just arrived at work, and I remember honestly thinking, "Man, I would really rather be in bed right now." My job is to encourage people and help others live out their best and healthiest life. Yet, I wasn't feeling so hot that day. PMS had hit me like a ton of bricks and the kids had challenged me from the moment they had woken up. We ended up being late to school and I got to work just feeling flustered and over the day before it even began.

But when I sat down to meet with a new client that morning, something inside of me shifted. This woman sat there, telling me about how she recently fell and hit her head and ended up in the emergency room, and how she got the scary news that at the rate her diabetes and health was going, it was only a matter of time until she had permanent, life-altering damage. Basically, she was told in more technical words that she was a "walking time bomb." Now, though she never expected to receive such shocking news she told me that she was glad she did. Because to her, it was the wakeup call she needed, and she felt as if she had been given a second chance at life. She then told me that she didn't really know where to start and she was looking for *me* to guide her and encourage her in learning to care for herself once again. What an incredible opportunity, right? I mean my job in general has always been rewarding but being given the opportunity to help someone make a comeback from a near-death experience takes it to a whole new level!

I know we already talked about how to clock in with a smile when your workplace isn't ideal but sometimes it has nothing to do with your environment and everything to do with *you*. In case you missed it, I currently love my job and love those I work with. I was in the perfect work setting that morning and I was being given the perfect opportunity to help someone in need. But, before I could help this woman, I knew that it was up to me to snap out of my funk and remember that God had placed me in that office on that Tuesday morning with that woman for a reason, and He needed me to show up and use my gifts to help her. It was up to me to look past myself and my frustrating morning and give back to someone God had placed in my path that day, even though I didn't feel like I had it in me.

A wise woman by the name of Madeline Bridges once said, *"Give the world the best you have, and the best will come back to you,"* and I couldn't agree more. I am a firm believer that when you give back to others, God will always bless you in return and, more often than not, I have discovered that blessing comes in the form of a renewed sense of purpose. I also believe that not a single person is ever placed in our path by mistake, and I knew this person was no different. God was asking me to use my gift of encouragement that day and even though I felt drained, it was up to me to choose obedience and show up for this woman regardless.

It's crazy cool how God can give us the strength we are lacking when we ask Him, isn't it? That day, and within five minutes into our consultation and after I quickly said a little prayer asking God for strength, I felt God give me the exact words I needed to teach this woman the lesson she needed to learn, in the exact way she needed to hear it. She left with a smile that day and a renewed sense of direction for the new year, and she texted me that night to let me know how much she appreciated me and my encouragement. She also told me that she was starting to feel excited about life once again for the first time in years. "Wow, just wow!" I thought.

After receiving her text, I remember freezing for a minute. I honestly couldn't believe how such a frazzled day had turned into such an amazing and rewarding day. And all simply because I decided to look beyond myself and utilize the gifts God gave me. That day I had arrived at work weary and ready to get my consultations over with, and God still used me to make a difference.

That night, after reading her text, my spirit was instantly lifted because I knew I had made a difference in someone else's life.

Okay, so let's talk about you, my friend, because you have God-given gifts as well. But in this chapter I am not necessarily referring to "gifts" as passions and hobbies of interest to you as we previously discussed, though they can be one in the same. I am referring to the specific gifts or talents God has given you that you can use to impact and help others around you. We all have them, so the question is what are they and how often do you use them to bless others?

If you are anything like me, you probably know what they are but you also probably don't always feel like using them. But I want you to know that if you are currently feeling this way, I get it. No, like, I really do. Sometimes, we just feel as if we have nothing left in us to give. We feel depleted and anxious about our lives, and we feel downright worn thin by the toll our day has placed on us.

I know what you are thinking. "Tell me *how*, Laura. How in the world am I supposed to make someone else smile when I can't bring myself to smile? How am I supposed to serve someone else today when I feel like such a hot mess?" Well, the answer is simple really. We have to first make sure we are putting our oxygen mask on so we have the energy to serve others (if you need a pep talk on this, check out my last book *Mama, You Still*

Matter); and then we need to pray for eyes to see and ears to hear those in need around us.

Think about Jesus as He walked this earth. He spent His days with those who seemingly, to the outside world, struggled the most. Yes, He spent time with prostitutes, beggars, lepers, you know, "those people." But do you think He ever got physically and emotionally tired of helping people? He was human, so I am guessing He probably did. Yet the fact still stands that He chose to go about His life encouraging and blessing others until the moment He was crucified. He chose to bless others and we are given the opportunity each day to do the same.

Someone, somewhere needs you to get out from underneath the covers and show up for them today. It may be someone in your very home. Yes, you may be snowed in and not even able to step foot outside of your house for days (I am currently snowed in, writing this chapter and believing that this book will impact the life of at least someone. So, here I am steadily typing along.) and God can still use you to make a profound difference in the life of your child or your spouse or maybe even someone on the other side of your screen (Hey! have you ever considered starting a blog or writing a book?). It may be someone in your workplace or in the grocery store checkout line. Really, it doesn't matter where you are. It just matters that you never stop striving to make an impact.

I know beyond a shadow of a doubt that God is waiting to use you in someone's life today. Whether your gift is in encouragement, leadership, baking or cooking, fixing a broken sink, assisting someone in their healing journey (whether it be physical, spiritual or mental), evangelism, teaching, nurturing, and so on, God is waiting on you to put your gifts to good use. You may not get the same rewarding text that I did that Tuesday at the end of every day giving you feedback about how you made a difference (and trust me, this isn't an everyday occurrence for me either). But just know that by showing up and using your gifts to serve others, you can find joy in the knowledge that you are acting as the hands and feet of Jesus and you are making this world a better place.

Giving back to the world by using your gifts is a guaranteed way to regain your joy and gain a new sense of purpose here on this earth. Don't we all want to feel that we are making a difference? I know I sure do! So, even on your worst day, I want you to keep in mind that you have the opportunity to make an impact, whether it be in the life of your child (I want to give a shoutout to every mama raising a little human or humans because you have one of the hardest but most rewarding jobs of all), your spouse's life, a coworker or friend's life, or that of a stranger. The sky and your mood may seem gray right now, your level of motivation may be close to none, tension in your life may be high, and your circumstances may seem bleak, but just remember that life is too darn short to stay under those covers! I will say it again. There is a reason God allowed you to wake up to a brand new day! So, why not thank God for giving you this day by choosing to really show up for it regardless of how it began? Whether it's a frazzled Tuesday or an easygoing Friday (TGIF!) let's make the conscious choice to get up, get going, and be a light!

DIVE DEEP:

- The enemy loves to steal your motivation. How can you keep Him from doing that?

- Someone, somewhere needs you to show up for them today so go find out who that is because they are waiting on you.

- Ask God to help you see each day as an opportunity to make a difference and a chance to be a light!

Taking Action Today

*"Don't talk, just act. Don't say, show.
Don't promise, prove."*
—*Unknown*

*"I want to change society's way of thinking in
regards to food and fitness."*
"I want to share my recipes."
"I want to encourage new mothers."
"I want to share my story."
"I want to write a book."

These were the dreams and goals I set for myself
years ago. Yet, for years I didn't really know how to
navigate my dreams. For the longest time, I didn't know
how to take action and so, for the longest time, I didn't.
It's not that I was lazy or without a vision. I knew in
my heart what I was meant to do but I was hesitant to
take the next step. I would blog here and there, and
I consulted part-time but deep down I knew in my heart
I was meant to do more.

One day, my sister-in-law gave me the nudge
I needed. We were sitting on her couch watching our
kids play when she gave me the suggestion to branch
out and start my own personal page on social media,

upgrade my blog, and share the recipes I had been creating for all those years behind the scenes. She's a very prestigious photographer and she offered to help me capture my recipes. It all sounded perfect. Yet, for a while, I tiptoed around her suggestion because I knew it would require me to take action and I knew it would require me to get out of my comfort zone. As much as I enjoyed creating and sharing my recipes and blogging about various health topics, it all came down to the fact that I truthfully just didn't want to put myself out into the spotlight.

Ironically, as much of a people person that I am, I really do prefer to stay behind the curtain. Maybe it's because deep down I fear judgment from others, or maybe it was because back then, I feared that no one would even bother to pay attention to a little blogger in Virginia. I mean, there were so many other more seemingly successful and sought-after bloggers and nutritionists on the web. "Why would anyone pay attention to me and what I had to offer and say?" I thought.

Self-doubt kept me from taking action for quite some time and because of that, I slowly felt my joy decrease. As we have already discussed, anytime we don't live up to our full potential we lose our spark, and that's exactly what was happening to me. I knew that when my sister-in-law had planted that seed, it was for a reason. I felt God calling me to take the next step and to take action and yet, I was afraid.

It wasn't until a few months went by of sitting on these ideas that I finally decided to bite the bullet. I hired a graphic designer to come up with my company logo, I created a new business Instagram and Facebook page, and I began organizing the list of recipes I wanted to share. A few weeks later I asked my super talented, artistic sister to help me stage my food during a photo shoot and my sister-in-law (the seed planter) to photograph my recipes and snap a couple of headshots for me while she was at it.

Little did I know that casual snapshot of me smiling down at a cutting board of colorful veggies would end up being the cover of my first book *Live Healthy With Laura*; little did I know that those recipes would end up being made and shared on the web by various followers I never expected to gain; and little did I know that by taking action, I would build the confidence I needed to pursue public speaking and write my second and third books. After I finally decided to get "unstuck," as I like to call it, doors that I never even imagined began to open for me.

Now, I know previously in the "No Thanks, I'll Pass" chapter we discussed how detrimental resisting change can be in our lives and how much it can impact our joy. But, in this chapter, I hope to take it a step further. You see, it's not just enough to wrap our head around the idea of change, we have to be willing to actually follow through and take action. Setting goals and making plans is always admirable. But let me ask you this: *When was the last time you actually took that next, faith-driven step?* When was the last time you set aside time to pursue something that you felt strongly you were meant to do?

Put actions behind your words, hopes, and dreams, my friend. You owe it to the Lord and to yourself to follow through with something that has been planted in your heart. But before we go any further, let's just take a moment to really think about the alternative. *How depressing would it be to get to the end of this year, only to look back and realize that you never achieved a single goal that you had set for yourself?* How disheartening would it be to have to face the fact that you held yourself back out of fear and because of that, you never took action? Take it from me, it's a pretty sucky place to be. But the exciting news, ladies and gentlemen, is that history does not have to repeat itself! You *can* take action starting TODAY! And fun fact: did you know that feeling of accomplishment, regardless of how small the goal, instantly releases dopamine, your "happy, go-getter" neurotransmitter? What that means is that if you break your dreams down into small, achievable steps then one by one, as you accomplish each goal, you will be more motivated to accomplish the next one! The hardest part, though, is always getting started.

So, why not bite the bullet and get the hard part over with? Stop holding yourself back and playing it safe. Life is too short for that and as we have already discussed, no one is promised tomorrow! Instead, why not take a leap of faith today and start by putting an action plan in place? *Remember, you have nothing to lose by taking the next step towards your dreams, but you have everything to lose by staying put where you are.* Could you use some more joy and excitement in your life? Well, then, make the conscious choice to get unstuck today and honor God with the dreams He has planted in your heart by taking action! Only by doing this can He entrust us with new opportunities and can we really start to see our dreams come to life!

DIVE DEEP:

- What specific goals and dreams has God planted in your heart?

- Are you currently taking action towards these personal goals and dreams or are they just sitting on the shelf?

- What is one practical way this week that you can take a step closer towards your life calling?

Health and Wellness Tips for a More Joyful You

As a nutritionist for almost ten years, I feel it's my duty to share with you a bit of what I know, starting with this: *how you treat your body can, in fact, impact your mood, mind, and ultimately, your perspective.* Though we may strive for a positive outlook on life, we won't be able to fully achieve that if we are depleted and stressed to the max. It just won't work. Our bodies and brains need to be cared for if we want to be able to process all the beauty around us. Period. Done. So, here are a few of my health and wellness tips to help you maintain a more joyful outlook as you go about your life. Even though a few may seem a bit random, I encourage you to give them a try because trust me, they really make a difference!

- *Don't skimp on sleep—you need seven to eight hours a night for a happy and healthy brain. Sleep is NOT optional if a happy and positive mood is your goal! Implement a calming evening routine that helps your brain disconnect from the day and be disciplined enough to go to bed at a decent hour.*
- *Drink organic coffee (it's proven to boost your happy, go-get-it-done neurotransmitter, dopamine)*

but stick to one cup before noon or else it can trigger anxiety and insomnia.

- *Indulge in dark chocolate (at least 65%) as it helps naturally boost one's serotonin levels (which is our happy and calming neurotransmitter) because it contains the amino acid tryptophan. It also has the power to lower blood pressure as well!*

- *Include lots of oranges, limes, and lemons in your diet. Doing this has been proven to boost one's overall mood. In fact, even just simply smelling citrus fruits has been shown to have an uplifting effect! I often diffuse citrus essential oils in my home for that reason (citrus oils do not trigger hormone imbalance as many other essential oils can) and especially in the winter (bye-bye winter blues)!*

- *When you can, let your bare feet touch the ground. This may sound super hippie, I know, but standing on the ground barefoot has been proven to help balance the negative and positive charges in your body and literally allow you to feel more calm and "grounded" (pun intended). Did you ever notice how you instantly seem to relax the second your feet hit the sand on the beach? That's why!*

- *Allow yourself to be lazy once in a while and unapologetically escape in an uplifting book or movie. Remember, our brains can't always be on! It's important sometimes to just have a designated day to relax, veg out, and unwind.*

- *Soak in a bath with about a cup of added magnesium chloride bath flakes for at least twenty minutes a couple times a week. This form of bath flakes is much more potent than regular Epsom salt and it naturally helps calm the nervous system as it increases the level of the calming mineral magnesium within the body. By soaking in magnesium chloride flakes (my favorite brand is Seven Minerals), it can almost instantly reach one's bloodstream and does not have to be broken down by our digestive tract and liver, which oftentimes can lessen the effect.*

- *Put your legs up the wall for ten minutes a day (this yoga pose is known as "Viparita Karani"), as this helps calm the central nervous system, which can then balance your mood and hormones. This also has been proven to help your adrenal glands recharge which could always use a little extra loving!*

- *Get moving somehow or some way every single day, as this boosts endorphins, which as you know (thanks to El Woods in Legally Blonde), "endorphins make you happy!" If you try a new workout and hate it, don't give up on exercising all together! Keep searching till you find one you enjoy!*

- *Eat more wild-caught salmon! Salmon is loaded with omega threes, which are proven to lower inflammation and boost our overall brain health and mood. It specifically also contains a good amount of the essential fatty acid, EPA, which has been shown to naturally lessen anxiety and depression. If you hate fish, talk to your doctor about starting on a high quality Omega 3 supplement (Solgar is my go-to brand).*

A Few Last Thoughts
on Perspective

A glass half full perspective? Yeah, it's unfortunately not just handed to us. But that doesn't mean we can't obtain it if we put in the work. Living out a "full life" requires positivity, thankfulness, and trust in our creator every day. It requires us to remember that nothing and no one ever comes into our path by mistake. It requires us to focus on what we do have and not so much on what we don't have. It requires us to sometimes get out of our comfort zone and take a leap of faith, change directions in our life, or move on from a toxic relationship. It may also require us to take a pause and think back over the past, and remind ourselves of all of the ways God has carried us through.

To live out our best, most joy-filled life, we have to sometimes disconnect from the world around us and calm the inner chaos within our minds. Then some days, we may feel the pull on our heart to consciously reconnect to the world around us and look for ways to use our gifts and ways to serve. When we do this, we have to also be on the lookout for the devil's attack, because as we have discussed, he wants nothing more than to extinguish our flame and plant seeds of doubt and insecurity within us. So, when this happens, we have to be ready to tell him to back the heck off and silence his voice. We also need to evaluate the voice within us and be willing to change the way we speak to ourselves. Yes, truly, this "glass half full perspective" thing can be an ever-changing and challenging journey, and it's one that we can't navigate alone.

Living a joy-filled life and maintaining a positive perspective isn't a three-step, easy process. Infact, sometimes it can feel like an uphill battle and, if you ask me, it actually takes a lot of work. But the work we put into it is so worth it, my friend! It's a daily battle that we *can* win if we ask God to help us see the light. We have the choice each and every day to ask God to reveal to us the beauty in our lives in a new and profound way. We also have the choice to ask God to help us not just see the light but *be* the light, and He has the power to give us what we ask.

When we look back through the Bible, time and time again we are reminded of God's truths. We are reminded that we are fearfully and wonderfully made and that we don't have to go through this life alone. We also are reminded that we weren't put on this earth to people please so therefore, we need to cut ourselves a break and stop trying so hard. We were made for a God-ordained purpose and we all have a life calling, regardless of what someone from your past or the voices in your head have told you. We are also reminded in the Bible that the devil (aka the "roaring lion") knows how valuable we are and He knows all that God has for us to do and therefore, wants nothing more than to tear us down. He wants nothing more than for us to see that glass as half empty and for us to see the world around us as gray.

But it's time to stop letting him skew our perspective, wouldn't you agree? This life is the one and only life you and I have to live. *So, I don't know about you, but I refuse to sit around any longer and complain about what I wish was filling my glass or what I wish wasn't* (as much as the devil eats that up). Instead, I want to live out each day choosing and chasing joy. I also want to remember that each day is an opportunity for new beginnings and each day is a gift. We aren't promised tomorrow but we have already been given today. So you better believe that I am going to slow down enough to not just look at and smell all of these gorgeous, pink roses surrounding me, but I am also going to stop and thank God for them, despite their thorns. Will you join me?